ANTIQUE Quilts & Textiles

A PRICE GUIDE TO

FUNCTIONAL AND FASHIONABLE CLOTH COMFORTS

Bobbie Aug
and
Gerald Roy

cb

COLLECTOR BOOKS

A Division of Schroeder Publishing Co., Inc.

ON THE COVER

From upper left in vertical rows:

Center Diamond with multiple Trips Around the World. Circa 1920, Pennsylvania, excellent condition. $1,500.00 – 1,800.00.

Detail of indigo, red, burgundy, and natural double weave wool and cotton coverlet. Circa 1850, excellent condition. $1,200.00 – 1,500.00.

Boy's navy blue woolen coat with white decorative cording design. Circa 1900, New England. $150.00.

Mennonite Indian Hatchet wool comfort. Circa 1900, Pennsylvania, excellent condition. $900.00 – 1,200.00.

Second row:

Reversible string-pieced Rocky Road to Kansas. Circa 1930, Midwest, excellent condition. $350.00 – 450.00.

Black wool petticoat with red quilting. Circa 1890, Pennsylvania, very good condition. $225.00 – 275.00.

Child's blue chambray dress with fancy lace collar for either boy or girl. Circa 1900, New England. $150.00.

Third row:

Show towel, white linen with colored cross-stitch, monogrammed. Dated 1830, Pennsylvania. $600.00 – 750.00.

Fourth row:

Blue gingham adult work bonnet. Fourth quarter nineteenth century, Pennsylvania. $125.00.

Cover design: Beth Summers
Book design: Holly C. Long
Editor: Gail Ashburn

Collector Books
P.O. Box 3009
Paducah, KY 42002-3009

www.collectorbooks.com

Copyright © 2004 Bobbie A. Aug & Gerald E. Roy

The current values in this book should be used only as a guide. They are not intended to set prices, which vary from one section of the country to another. Auction prices as well as dealer prices vary greatly and are affected by condition and demand. Neither the authors nor the publisher assumes responsibility for any losses which might be incurred as a result of consulting this guide.

Searching For A Publisher?

We are always looking for people knowledgeable within their fields. If you feel there is a real need for a book on your collectible subject and have a large comprehensive collection, contact Collector Books.

Contents

Acknowledgments

We would like to thank the following friends: Dawn Heefner for allowing us to photograph the most wonderful girl's bonnet. Faye Foster for her assistance with the children's clothing and linens, which made this book journey so much easier. Don Leiby for his continued friendship, support, and contribution to our world of collecting.

It is important to acknowledge the fervor and joy with which the late Paul D. Pilgrim celebrated the past. Without his collection of textiles, this book would not have been possible. Thank you, Paul.

Preface

This is a comprehensive guide to collecting antique textiles compiled by quilt historians and appraisers Bobbie Aug and Gerald Roy. Both authors have written other books and articles and curated exhibits featuring antique textiles. In general, age, pattern, style, size, fabrics, colors, construction techniques, workmanship, and current lack of availability were the criteria used in valuing the various articles in this guide. Any other criterion, specific to the individual item, has been duly noted in the appropriate section.

Nearly all of the items illustrated and valued were purchased by the authors and are currently, or were at one time, in their private collections. So, with very few exceptions, we bought everything you see on these pages and we feel our experiences in the marketplace better enable us to present reliable information to you, the collector.

The values in this book are retail values and should be used only as a guide. They are not intended to set prices, which vary from one region of the country to another and are affected by the condition of the textile as well as supply and demand and the local, national, and world economy. The only true guide to determining value is between a buyer and a seller. Neither the authors nor the publisher assume responsibility for any losses that might be incurred as a result of consulting this guide.

Introduction

The need for warm covering was a motive for cloth manufacture and the impetus for creating necessary quilts, coverlets, other bed coverings, and clothing. We have chosen a comprehensive selection of cloth comforts currently of interest in the marketplace, specifically, aprons, bonnets, comforts, coverlets, fabric, petticoats, quilts, quilt tops, rugs, socks, spreads, and towels.

We have collected or compiled information that, hopefully, will allow you to familiarize yourself with both commonplace and fancy items referenced and assessed for today's market. Our goal was to provide a source to guide and educate the inexperienced buyer about currently popular collectibles and provide a resource for appraisers and others interested in current market values. Many of the common articles of the past are rare and unusual today and that is an important factor when determining value. These values reflect either our own experiences in the marketplace as buyers/collectors, or the research we have conducted.

This book presents a selection of textiles from both the nineteenth and twentieth centuries, representative of art and function of everyday living. These artifacts, even those that represent the simplest utilitarian objects of everyday life, contain the feelings and the romance that we associate with the past. They also represent an appreciation today that did not exist during their own period in history. Through time, we have come to not only appreciate their practical value, but we recognize the time, energy, and creativity of the maker to produce objects not only for necessity but for artistic expression.

Collecting in General

The age of a textile, whether it's a quilt, coverlet, or some type of clothing, can affect value. We are drawn to old textiles because of our love of history and our ability to romanticize about life long ago. We cherish these pieces because we know that they won't last forever and need to be respected and well taken care of. Our ability to visualize what the textile once looked like when it was new makes our "find" even more exciting. However, please consider the following:

Condition is of the utmost importance. You can expect to pay more for textiles in excellent condition than ones in poor condition. Most experienced collectors prefer to buy pieces in excellent condition; thereby eliminating the time, money, and effort of extensive restoration. Buy articles in the best condition that you can possibly afford.

Workmanship is another important consideration. Something poorly made a hundred years ago is still poorly made — the workmanship doesn't get better with age. Like condition, you can expect to pay more for a textile with excellent workmanship than one with poor workmanship. Again, buy examples of the best workmanship you can afford.

Look for articles that best represent the function and fashion that you are collecting. Make sure that you have examples that can be easily identified with whatever your focus is: time period, color, trend, etc. Then, look for articles that are somewhat unusual within your category of collecting — some little unique pattern or detail that adds interest and character. Some of the best collections have been built around quirky characteristics.

After you have narrowed down your specific category for collecting, such as quilts or clothing, there are other decisions to make. You might focus on a particular religious sect such as Amish, Mennonite, or Quaker. Perhaps who the textile was intended for would be of interest to you such as doll or crib quilts or clothing for children. Or, the intended use such as for the bed which could include pillowcases, woven coverlets, comforters, bed linens, etc.

Construction technique is another way to group your articles. Embroidered, appliquéd, woven are just a few methods that could be used to define your collection.

Consider the care and storage of the textiles you wish to collect. Some fibers attract insects, such as moths to wool, and this is an important consideration when deciding what to collect. If you wish to exhibit or display your collection, think about what would be easiest for you to manage in the space available to you. Textiles with strong visual appeal might be more attractive in your display space. A textile collection of even a few quilts should be covered by insurance. Companies who write homeowner's insurance vary in the amount of coverage provided in the basic plan. Check with your insurance agent to make sure your collection is protected.

A qualified appraiser of textiles should be contacted to prepare an appraisal for each of the quilts in your collection. A knowledgeable appraiser should also be able to evaluate your quilts as a collection.

Safe Storage

Storage must be arranged for your textile collection. All textiles need to be protected from insects, acids, dust, light, and stress. Air circulation should be provided. Storage should be in an area with even, moderate humidity and temperature (not the attic or the basement). Embrittlement is very destructive and can be avoided or postponed for decades. This condition is caused by great fluctuation of temperature, humidity, and pollution in the air, sunlight, and soil. If textiles are stored in an area with high humidity, check often for signs of mold and mildew. Overly dry conditions can cause dehydration and breakage of the fibers. When a humidifier is needed for humans, textiles will benefit as well.

Cleanliness and good housekeeping will insure that no pests get into your textiles. Food stains and other soil provide nutrients for insects and mold. Mothballs and other chemicals are no longer recommended because they can cause damage to textiles and are toxic to humans. If mothballs are the only remedy available to you, enclose them in cloth bags and do not let them come in direct contact with the cloth. Cedar, another popular home remedy, does not provide a safe deterrent to insects. Cedar is also bare wood and a source of acid deterioration for any fabric stored on its surface. Monitor pest activity on a regular schedule with your usual cleaning.

When folding textiles for storage, sheets of acid-free paper should be placed between the layers of the item and scrunched up in the folds in order to prevent the textile from touching itself and prevent "pancake" folds or creases in the textile. Fold the item into the size that will fit on a finished shelf or in a finished cabinet. Cover the shelf with unbleached muslin or acid-free tissue paper. Refold the textile about every three months. Do not stack items. The weight of one textile on top of another can be stressful. Garments need to have acid free paper lining as well as padding in shoulder and sleeve areas to keep creases from forming and alleviate stress.

Acid-free storage boxes can be purchased from archival storage materials suppliers. These are opaque, expensive, and need to be replaced about every three to five years. In semi-arid regions such as Nevada, Arizona, and Colorado, textiles can safely be stored in polypropylene or polyethylene (plastic) storage containers. This type of material is inert and will not give off harmful gasses that could damage textiles. Unbleached muslin is used to loosely line the container in order to wick out any moisture that might have accumulated on the item or in the box. The tops of these containers are not air-tight, so circulation is provided. The sizes available include under bed storage, small textiles size as well as containers to accommodate large quilts, comforts, and coverlets. The boxes can be stacked and no damage occurs to the fabrics.

Rolling textiles for storage saves space and is more economical than purchasing acid-free boxes. Probably for these reasons, museums frequently roll quilts around dowel rods or carpet tubes attached to the wall. Rolling, however, puts tension on every square inch of the cloth. In addition, in quilted or stuffed items, the batting is pulled to one side of the quilted area and visually distorts the surface of the textile. We recommend avoiding rolling if at all possible.

Glossary

To pattern: Quilting stitches are ¼" inside the seam and the quilting echoes the patchwork pattern.

By the piece: Same as to pattern.

Baptist Fan: Concentric arcs. This pattern is sometimes referred to as elbow qulting or shell quilting. See Pickle Dish on page 32 for an example.

The Quilts

CLOTH

Originally, woven cloth was for protection from the elements and for warmth and security. Eventually cloth became decorative when the warp was combined with a different color weft, and a geometric design or pattern resulted. This probably was the beginning of the industry we recognize today.

Techniques applying design on the surface of woven cloth soon followed. This allowed freedom from woven geometric patterns to unlimited design possibilities. Simple stamping or block printing was the first method of transferring color to the surface of cloth. At this point the simple aspect of maintaining the design on the cloth becomes necessary. Experimentation with pigments and mordant was necessary to achieve permanence of design. With improved technology came more sophisticated combinations of color and pattern and technique.

From the infancy stage of cloth production, it represented status and luxury. For some, its purpose was strictly utilitarian, but for others with wealth and station, it also served to increase enjoyment and as personal decoration.

Through history, fabrics have always reflected fashion styles and trends of the time in which they were produced. The evolution of design, the immense variety of color and pattern, the recognition of an industry that presents beautiful works of art, and the contribution to documentation of our history in this unique form is why textile historians, museums, costume collectors, and historical societies are interested in gathering these cloth artifacts.

Cloth has a relatively short lifespan compared to other objects. As a result, there is only a small representation from the past. This scarcity automatically creates a healthy market, i.e. demand. However, collecting antique fabric is less expensive than purchasing quilts and other large textiles. It is more practical to store and yet it satisfies the need for those who respond to the tactile sensuality of cloth.

Some people are drawn to collecting antique fabric just because of the sheer beauty of cloth; others are interested in fabrics because of historical or political significance, or perhaps novelty prints, special techniques such as woven designs, finishes, or prints, style (art deco, floral, toile, etc.), or a particular time period.

It is important to note that America, England, and France all copied prints from one another. Fabrics were reproduced, almost from the beginning of the mechanized printing industry. Often, the changes that were made to the reproduction fabrics were so subtle that it is extremely difficult to tell which is the original older piece and which is the reproduction. In some cases, there were no changes — printing companies would reprint the same patterns exactly as they had been decades earlier. These practices can cause confusion and difficulty when determining the date of textiles.

QUILTS

Quilted textiles are as old as recorded history. Archaeologists have found evidence in burial sites dating back many thousands of years. It would seem that every culture, needing protection from the cold, discovered the benefits of layers of cloth sewn together to provide an insulating covering. In every case, not only was the found example utilitarian, but also some attempt at artistry was also present. It would appear that as in many other kinds of household tools, the surface of a quilted article was also recognized as a surface to be adorned.

It is this that draws us to quilts today. They appear to attract us because of their beauty in color, design, and workmanship. However, as we become more deeply involved in the history of these textiles, we begin to realize the depth and enrichment these pieces of cloth provide, with regards to their importance as part of our material culture.

Quilts provide a wide variety of reasons to collect. The current interest in nostalgia in our country has added to the popularity of collecting and decorating with antique quilts. As a general guide to the values that we have researched and recorded, you will find that Amish and Mennonite quilts, unique or unusual patterns or sets, age, size, unusual techniques or combinations of techniques, intricate and/or difficult patterns to execute, and quilts that are visually very exciting and pleasing reflected these qualities in their values. In your study and research of antique quilt values, you may find that blue quilts are valued higher than pink quilts. Star patterns were among the first pieced quilt patterns and remain very popular. Log Cabin is another popular style or pattern that is very collectible. Houses or Double Wedding Ring might be more exciting than Churn Dash, while whole cloth trapunto would be valued higher than cross-stitch. Because of all of the other criteria involved in determining the appropriate fair market value, it is unwise to generalize values when considering specific quilts. In other words, examine each quilt you are considering buying carefully; determine what the strong and weak points are and whether it is priced accordingly. Buy what you like and buy the best condition you can afford.

The Quilts

When determining appropriate values for the quilted textiles in this book, we relied on sales statistics for comparable properties. This included published auction sale results, sales at national vendor markets at major quilt show venues, local and regional antique malls, and personal experiences selling and buying antique quilts. We did not consider any Internet sources as we were not aware of any reliable documentation prior to completion of this book. We also considered the state of our national economy at the time this book went to print. The stock market was on a steady rise, but consumers were being somewhat guarded about buying big-ticket items.

Appliquéd Quilts

A

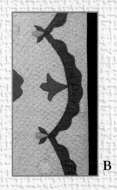

B

C

Lancaster Rose appliqué. Cotton. Hand appliquéd, hand quilted. Quilting: to pattern, grid in blocks, diamond grid in border. Cotton batt. Applied white straight grain binding. Muslin back. Circa 1850, Lancaster, Pennsylvania, 73" x 96", excellent condition. $2,500.00 – 2,800.00.
A. Detail of block
B. Detail of border
C. Detail of corner

A

Center medallion appliqué with evening stars surround. Leaf and rose appliquéd border. Cotton. Hand pieced, hand appliquéd, hand quilted. Quilting: heavily quilted, to pattern in the blocks, crosshatch or grid between blocks, and diagonal grid and to pattern in the border. Cotton batt. Applied white straight grain binding. Muslin back. Circa 1850, Pennsylvania, 84" x 96", excellent condition. $2,600.00 – 2,800.00.
A. Detail
B. Detail

B

Trailing Ivy center medallion kit. Leaves, vines, and tendrils are embroidered. Cotton. Hand appliquéd, hand quilted, hand embroidered. Quilting: to pattern, sunburst center, feather swags, and parallel lines on the border and scallop shell in each radius corner. Cotton batt. Green bias applied binding. Muslin back. Circa 1940, Pennsylvania, 72" x 88", excellent condition. $800.00 – 1,000.00.

A. Detail of medallion

A

A

North Carolina Lily. Cotton. Hand appliquéd, hand pieced, hand quilted. Quilting: to pattern, grid and cable in sashing. Cotton batt. Applied pink straight binding. Muslin back. Circa 1940, Pennsylvania, 72" x 88", excellent condition. $600.00 – 700.00.

A. Detail of block

Pieced Quilts

B

Whole cloth chintz cut out four poster with attached ruffle skirt. Cotton. Beautifully hand quilted. Quilting: lattice on point. Cotton batt. Corded edge finish. Skirt gathered and attached at cording. Ombre stripe with floral and leaf motif back. Circa 1830, Massachusetts, 92" x 94", excellent condition. $4,200.00 – 4,800.00.

A. Detail
B. Detail of backing

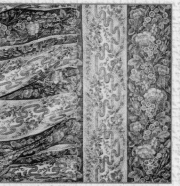

A

Indigo and white pieced Feathered Star. Cotton. Hand pieced, heavily hand quilted. Quilting: to pattern, with chevron designs in alternate blocks, double rodding. Cotton batt. Applied straight grain indigo binding. Muslin back. Circa 1840, New England, 76" x 92", some wear and binding is frayed. $675.00 – 800.00.
A. Detail of block
B. Detail of back

A

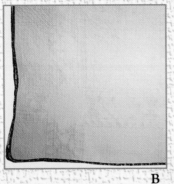

B

Friendship Album. 12½" blocks sashed and set on point. Signatures signed or stamped in ink on blocks and some dated 1847. Cotton. Hand pieced, hand quilted. Quilting: diagonal parallel lines in blocks, sashing is quilted in double vertical rows. Cotton batt. Applied straight grain binding. Brown plaid back. 1847, 80" x 93", fair condition. $700.00 – 900.00.
A. Detail of block
B. Detail of back

A

B

A

B

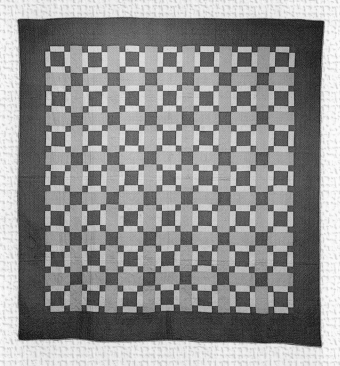

A

B

Top:
LeMoyne Star. Cotton. Hand pieced, hand quilted. Quilting: to pattern in blocks, interlocking circles in alternate blocks, grape vine and leaf in border with parallel lines and clamshells in border. Cotton batt. White straight grain applied binding. Muslin back. Circa 1830, Pennsylvania, 128" x 128", good condition, some staining. $1,200.00 – 1,500.00.
　　　A. Detail of blocks
　　　B. Detail of border

Bottom:
Puss in the Corner. Cotton. Hand pieced, hand quilted. Quilting: floral patterns in blocks, alternate blocks, and sashing, straight grid in border. Cotton batt. Pink applied straight grain binding. Whole cloth printed large polka dot back. Circa 1840, Lancaster County, Pennsylvania, 86" x 90", excellent condition. $1,200.00 – 1,500.00.
　　　A. Detail of blocks
　　　B. Detail of back

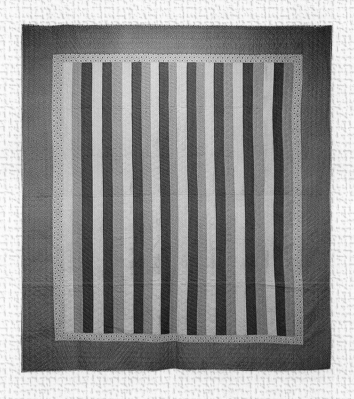

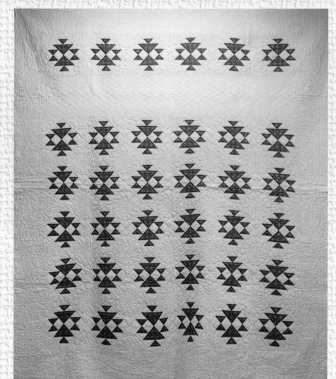

Top:
Bars. Documented in the Berks County Documentation Project. Cotton. Came from the Kramer family. Machine pieced, hand quilted. Quilting: to pattern, cable, and grid. Cotton batt. Applied blue straight grain binding. Blue back same as binding. Circa 1870, Pennsylvania, 83" x 92", excellent condition. $1,500.00 – 1,800.00.

Bottom:
Double X. Blocks set 6 x 5 on main area of quilt. Six blocks across top section for pillow area. Cotton. Hand pieced, hand quilted. Quilting: to pattern, floral, diagonal grid. Cotton batt. Applied white straight grain binding. Whole cloth muslin back. Circa 1860, New England, 78" x 96", excellent condition. $650.00 – 850.00.

A. Detail of block

A

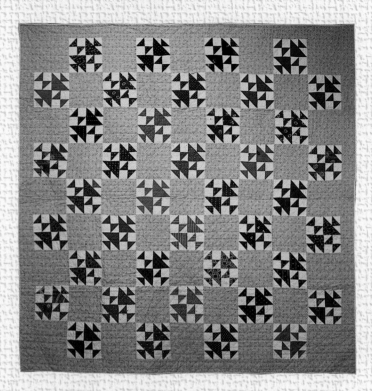

A

B

A

Top: Old Maid's Puzzle. Cotton. Hand and machine pieced, hand quilted. Quilting: allover diagonal grid. Cotton batt. Back brought around to front. Muslin back. Circa 1880, Pennsylvania, 74" x 76", excellent condition. $550.00 – 650.00.

    A. Detail of blocks
    B. Detail of back

Bottom: Hourglass in bars setting with Sawtooth border. Red and white. Cotton. Hand and machine pieced, hand quilted. Quilting: to pattern, diagonal grid in blocks and cable in the border. Cotton batt. Applied muslin straight grain binding. Muslin back. Circa 1880, New England, 85" x 89", excellent condition. $700.00 – 900.00.

    A. Detail of border

Top: T Block — similar to Four T's pattern. Red and white cotton. Hand pieced, hand quilted. Quilting: sparsely quilted to pattern. Cotton batt. Red applied straight grain binding. Muslin back. Circa 1910, Manchester, New Hampshire, 71" x 73", poor condition. $250.00 – 300.00.
A. Detail of block

Bottom: Center Diamond with multiple Trips Around the World. Cotton. Hand-pieced, hand quilted. Quilting: 2½" grid on point in outer border, 1½" straight grid throughout the center of the quilt. Cotton batt. Red applied straight grain binding. Printed back. Circa 1920, Pennsylvania, 81" x 83", excellent condition. $1,500.00 – 1,800.00.
A. Detail
B. Detail
C. Detail of back and binding

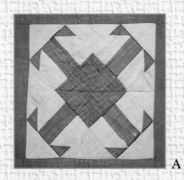

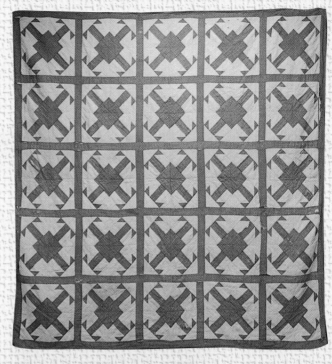

A

A

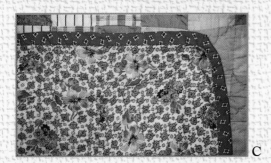

C

A

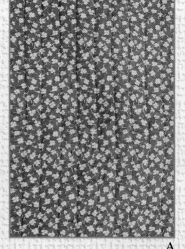

A

Top: Stars of Bethlehem, sashed and corner blocked. Cotton. Hand and machine pieced, hand quilted. Quilting: 1" and ½" grid on point. Cotton batt. Blue applied straight grain binding. Printed back. Circa 1880, Pennsylvania, 75" x 78", excellent condition. $900.00 – 1,200.00.

    A. Detail of block

Bottom: Lone Star with small stars in corners and partial stars in setting triangles. Pieced Dogtooth border, top and bottom. Cotton. Hand pieced and hand quilted. Quilting: diagonal parallel lines. Cotton batt. Blue on top and white on sides applied straight grain binding. Purple and white floral print back. Circa 1945, 64" x 78", excellent condition. $800.00 – 1,000.00.

    A. Detail of back

A

B

Top: LeMoyne Stars with appliquéd stars in border. Cotton. Hand pieced, hand quilted. Quilting: diagonal parallel lines, crosshatch on point, ¼" inside diamonds. Cotton batt. Applied straight grain binding. Muslin back. Circa 1870, New England, 74" x 88", good condition. $900.00.
A. Detail
B. Detail

Bottom: Star of Bethlehem with chevron backgrounds. Cotton. Hand pieced and hand quilted. Quilting: Baptist Fan throughout. Cotton batt. Green applied straight grain binding. Muslin back. Circa 1900, Missouri, 79" x 80", very good condition, minor fading. $1,000.00 – 1,200.00.
A. Detail

A

A

B

A

Top: Colonial Girl. Multicolored embroidery on white ground. Merribee Art Embroidery Company, pattern dated 1924. Cotton. Hand embroidered, hand quilted. Quilting: cable in border, 1" grid on point in interior. Cotton batt. Knife edge finish. Muslin back. Circa 1924, 65" x 86", excellent condition. $350.00 – 450.00.

    A. Detail of embroidery
    B. Detail of pillow area

Bottom: Embroidered Peacocks. Multicolored embroidery on white ground. Merribee Art Embroidery Company, pattern dated 1924. Cotton. Hand embroidered, hand quilted. Quilting: interlocking circles with a fern frond border. Cotton batt. Knife edge finish. Muslin back. Circa 1924, Pennsylvania, 70" x 85", excellent condition. $350.00 – 450.00.

    A. Detail of embroidery

A

Top: Boudoir quilt. Pink acetate. Hand quilted, trapunto. Quilting: cables, echo, diagonal parallel lines, urns with roses and leaves. Each corner of the inner frame has a rose flanked by leaves. Cotton batt. Scalloped edge with applied bias binding. Gray acetate back. Circa 1920, 54" x 72", excellent condition. $450.00 – 550.00.
A. Detail of center

Bottom: Yoyo coverlet. Complex center medallion arrangement. Cotton. Hand assembled. No batt. No backing. Circa 1940, Pennsylvania, 78" x 92", excellent condition. $800.00 – 1,000.00.
A. Detail of center
B. Detail
C. Detail of border

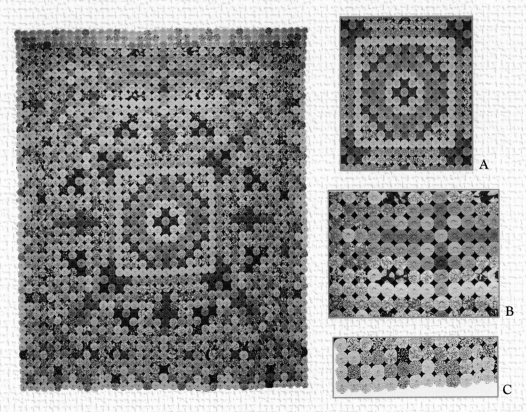

A

B

C

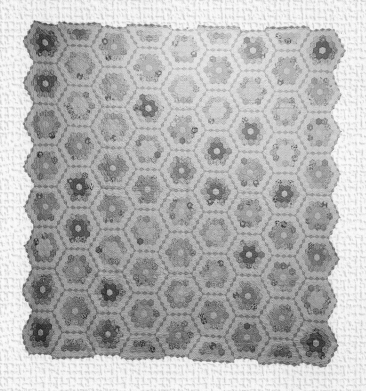

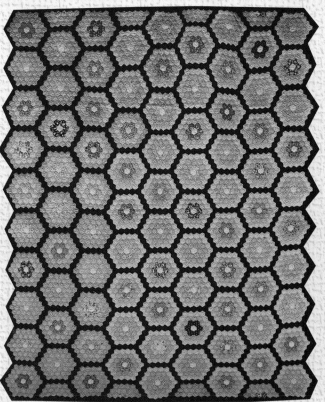

A

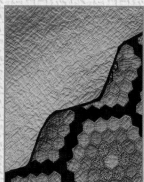

B

Top left: Grandmother's Flower Garden. Cotton. Hand pieced, hand quilted. Quilting: to pattern. Cotton batt. Applied bias binding. Muslin back. Circa 1940, Pennsylvania. $650.00 – 750.00.

Top right: Grandmother's Flower Garden. Cotton. Top is hand appliquéd onto pink borders, hand pieced, hand quilted. Quilting: to pattern in patchwork, diagonal grid in borders. Cotton batt. Green applied bias binding. Circa 1940, Pennsylvania, 78" x 94", excellent condition. $550.00 – 650.00.

Bottom: Pink and black Grandmother's Flower Garden. Cotton. Unusual black setting hexagons between flowers. Hand pieced, hand quilted. Quilting: by the piece. Cotton batt. Applied bias binding. Pink back. Circa 1930, Kentucky, 62" x 79", excellent condition. $650.00.

A. Detail of block
B. Detail of back

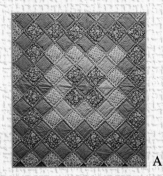

A

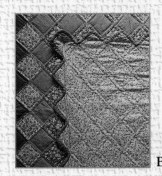

B

C

Top: Grandmother's Dream or Sunshine and Shadows. Cotton. Hand pieced, hand quilted. Quilting: to pattern. Cotton batt. Green applied bias binding. Floral print back. Circa 1940, 86" x 88", excellent condition. $650.00 – 800.00.

A. Detail of center
B. Detail of back and binding
C. Detail of corner

Right: Cheater cloth. Cotton. Hand quilted. Quilting: good Baptist Fans quilting throughout. Cotton batt. Front brought to back edge finish. Black mourning print back. Circa 1890, Pennsylvania, 72" x 78", excellent condition. $500.00.

A. Detail of corner
B. Detail of back and binding

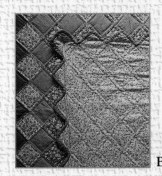

A

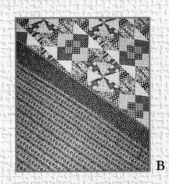

B

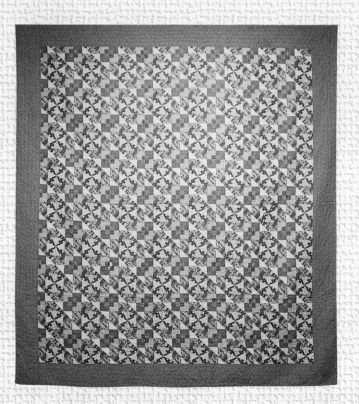

The Quilts – Pieced Quilts

Top left: Double Wedding Ring with unusual striped fabric in the piecing. Cotton. Hand pieced, hand quilted. Quilting: eight lobed design elements in centers with variation of that design in other places. Excellent workmanship. Cotton batt. White applied straight binding. Muslin back. Circa 1940, 70" x 84", excellent condition. $1,000.00 – 1,200.00.

A. Detail

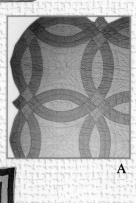

Above: Double Wedding Ring on tan ground. Cotton. Hand pieced and quilted. Quilting: flower and leaves in centers, interlocking rings in melons, and to pattern. Cotton batt. Pink applied bias binding. Yellow back. Circa 1930, 77" x 90", excellent condition. $700.00 – 900.00.

A. Detail

Bottom: Double Wedding Ring. Cotton. Hand pieced, hand quilted. Quilting: to pattern, four lobed medallion centers, echo, and cable in the borders. Cotton batt. Yellow applied straight grain binding. Muslin back. Circa 1940, 65" x 81", excellent condition. $450.00 – 550.00.

A. Detail

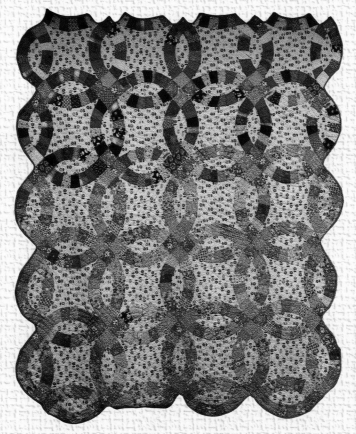

A

Top: Double Wedding Ring with floral print ground. Cotton. Hand pieced, hand quilted. Quilting: Baptist Fan quilting throughout. Cotton batt. Red applied bias front facing. Knife edge finish. Muslin back. Circa 1930, 76" x 88", excellent condition. $750.00 – 950.00.
A. Detail

Bottom: Double Wedding Ring on black and white shirting print ground. Cotton. Hand pieced, hand quilted. Quilting: ½" inside to pattern, curved parallel lines, echo. Cotton batt. Green straight grain applied binding. Green back. Circa 1920, 80" x 82", excellent condition. $800.00 – 1,000.00.
A. Detail
B. Detail of back

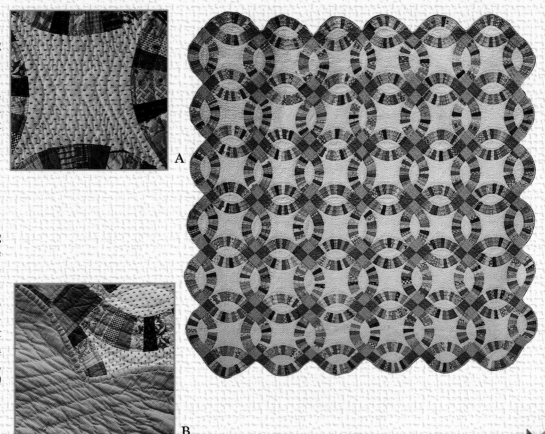
A

B

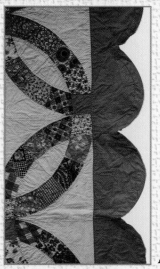

A

A

Top: Double Wedding Ring with purple ruffle. Cotton. Hand and machine pieced, hand quilted. Quilting: to pattern. No batting. Purple bias applied binding. White back. Circa 1940, 76" x 90", excellent condition. $450.00 – 550.00.

A. Detail of border

Bottom: Double Wedding Ring with pink footballs. Cotton. Hand pieced, hand quilted. Quilting: diamond crosshatch, ¼" inside to pattern. Cotton batt. White applied bias binding. White back. Circa 1930, 74" x 89", excellent condition. $500.00 – 650.00.

A. Detail

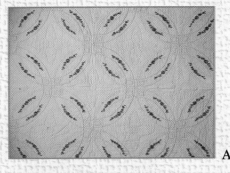

A

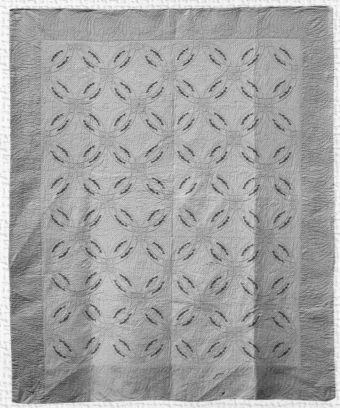

B

Top: Embroidered Double Wedding Ring on white ground. Signed Ivy M. Renner, North Hampton, Pennsylvania, 1940. Cotton. Hand embroidered, hand quilted, machine pieced. Quilting: crosshatch in center blocks, stylized floral border. Cotton batt. Front to back edge finish. Yellow back. 1940, 74" x 92", excellent condition. $650.00 – 800.00.
A. Detail
B. Detail of embroidery

Bottom: Amish Trip Around the World. Silk crepe, acetate. Machine pieced, hand quilted in black thread. Quilting: feathers and vines, crosshatch grid. Cotton batt. Purple applied straight grain binding. Printed nylon and cotton back. Circa 1950, Leola, Pennsylvania, 87" x 87", excellent condition. $2,500.00 – 2,700.00.
A. Detail of center
B. Detail of border
C. Detail of back

A

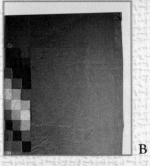

B

C

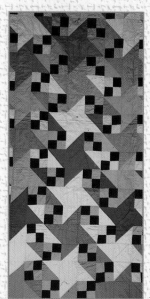

A

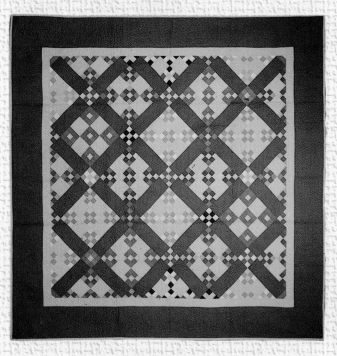

Top: Amish Water Wheel. Polished cotton. Machine pieced, hand quilted in green thread. Quilting: to pattern. Cotton batt. Dark blue applied straight grain binding. Green polished cotton back. Circa 1940, Mifflin County, Pennsylvania, 78" x 88", excellent condition. $2,800.00 – 3,500.00.
A. Detail of center

Bottom: Amish Double Nine Patch, on point and sashed with Nine Patch at intersections. Cotton. Machine pieced, hand quilted. Quilting: to pattern and cable. Cotton batt. Beige applied straight grain binding. Muslin back. Circa 1970, Holmes County, Ohio, 84" x 84", excellent condition. $2,200.00 – 2,600.00.
A. Detail of corner, border, and binding

A

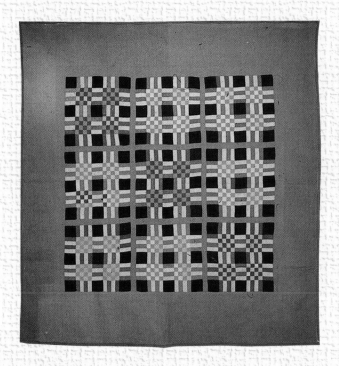

Top left: Amish Sixteen Patch and Rails. Cotton plain weave and cotton sateen. Machine pieced, hand quilted in black thread. Quilting: diagonal grid through blocks, cable in inner frame, and fern frond border. Cotton batt. Blue back brought to front. Blue cotton back. Circa 1935, Mifflin County, Pennsylvania, 76" x 82", fair condition, some wear and fading. $1,500.00 – 1,800.00.

Top right: Mennonite Joseph's Coat. Cotton. Machine pieced, hand quilted. Quilting: cable in border, double grid on point in interior. Cotton batt. Red applied straight grain binding. Whole cloth tiny dots printed back. Circa 1880, Pennsylvania, 82" x 86", excellent condition. $5,400.00 – 6,000.00.
A. Detail of corner and binding

Bottom: Mennonite Double Irish Chain. Cotton. Machine pieced, hand quilted. Quilting: to pattern and grid on point. Medallion design in green. Cotton batt. Dark green print applied straight grain binding. Whole cloth printed back. Circa 1880, Pennsylvania, 74" x 86", excellent condition. $1,800.00 – 2,200.00.
A. Detail of back and binding

A

A

B

Top: Mennonite Ocean Waves. Cotton. Machine pieced, hand quilted. Quilting: floral, to pattern, grid on point, cable in borders. Cotton batt. Front brought to back. Small geometric print back. Circa 1880, Pennsylvania, excellent condition. $2,800.00 – 3,500.00.

    A. Detail of corner

Bottom: Ocean Waves. Cotton. Machine pieced, hand quilted. Quilting: cable on border, to pattern, grid on point, chevron. Cotton batt. White applied straight grain binding. Muslin back. Circa 1890, Pennsylvania, 84" x 86", excellent condition. $650.00 – 750.00.

    A. Detail of block
    B. Detail of corner

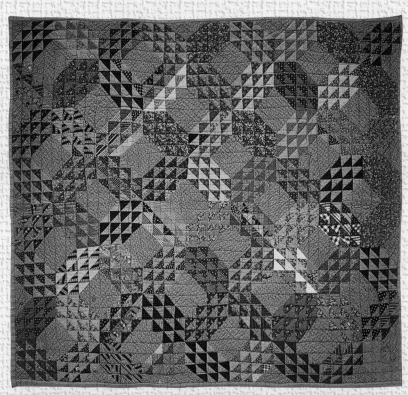

Top: Ocean Waves. Cotton. Hand pieced, hand quilted. Quilting: to pattern, straight grid. Cotton batt. Brown applied straight grain binding. Brown print back. Circa 1890, Indiana, excellent condition. $900.00 – 1,200.00.

Bottom: Amish or Mennonite Fan. Cotton. Hand and machine pieced, hand embroidered, hand quilted in green thread. Quilting: to pattern, fern frond in border. Cotton batt. Green wide unfilled (Amish style) straight grain applied binding. Solid pink back. Circa 1940, Pennsylvania, 84" x 87", excellent condition. $600.00 – 700.00.
A. Detail of corner

A

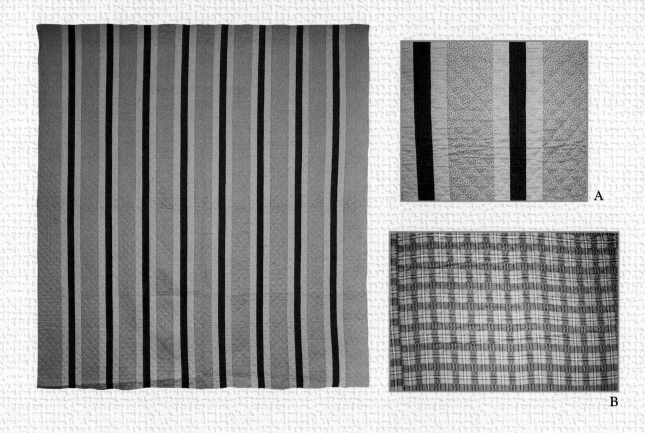

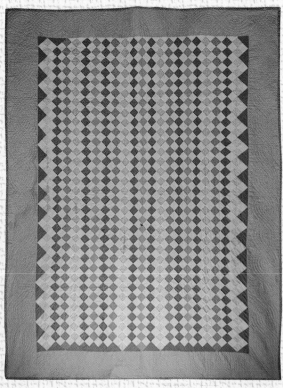

A

B

A

B

Top: Mennonite Bars. Cotton. Machine pieced, hand quilted. Quilting: crosshatch on point throughout. Cotton batt. Front to back edge finish. Brown and white plaid twill weave back. Circa 1880, Pennsylvania, 86" x 92", excellent condition. $800.00 – 1,000.00.

A. Detail
B. Detail of back

Bottom: Mennonite Postage Stamp in vertical set. Cotton. Hand and machine pieced, hand quilted. Quilting: to pattern, cable on border. Cotton batt. Green print applied straight grain binding. Brown and white print back. Circa 1880, Pennsylvania, excellent condition. $900.00 – 1,200.00.

A. Detail of corner
B. Detail of binding and back

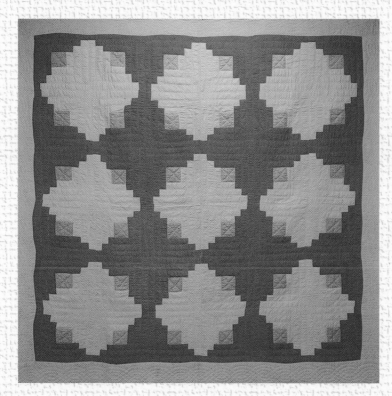

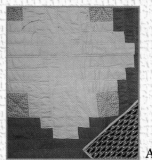

A

Top: Mennonite Log Cabin Dark and Light. Cotton. Machine pieced, hand quilted. Quilting: to pattern, "X" through blue centers, cable in border. Cotton batt. Orange applied straight grain binding. Pink, black, and white print back. Circa 1880, Oley Valley, Pennsylvania, 82" x 82", excellent condition. $650.00 – 800.00.
A. Detail of back and binding

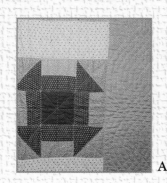

A

Bottom: Mennonite Hole in the Barn Door. Cotton. Machine pieced, hand quilted. Quilting: wedges in corner posts, blocks also divided with horizontal, vertical, and diagonal lines, cables in border, parallel lines in sashing. Cotton batt. Pink applied straight grain binding. Red and blue pieced bars back. Circa 1880, Pennsylvania, 63" x 80", excellent condition. $700.00 – 900.00.
A. Detail
B. Detail of back

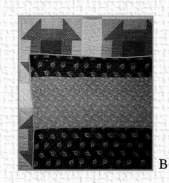

B

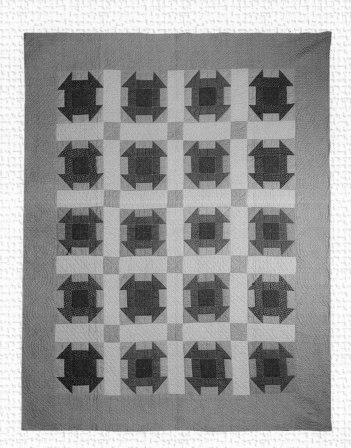

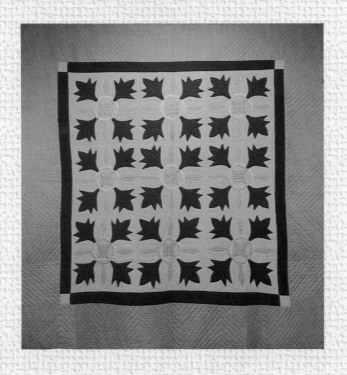

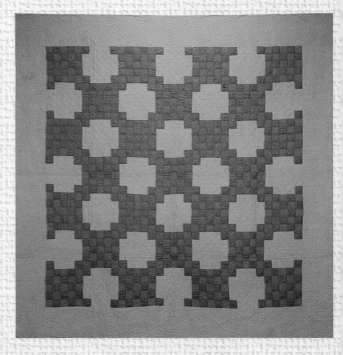

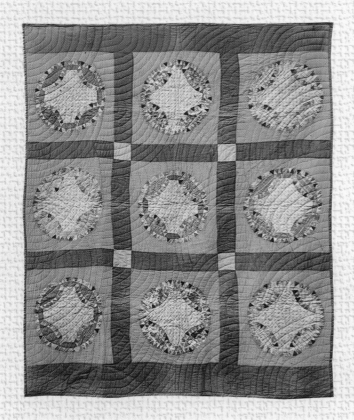

Top left: Mennonite Oakleaf and Reel. Cotton. Machine pieced, hand appliquéd, hand quilted. Quilting: to pattern, diagonal grid and chevron in borders. Cotton batt. Pink applied straight grain binding. Pink back. Circa 1880, Pennsylvania, excellent condition. $900.00 – 1,200.00.

Top right: Mennonite Triple Irish Chain. Cotton. Machine pieced, hand quilted. Quilting: to pattern, diagonal grid, cable in border. Cotton batt. Orange applied straight grain binding. Cotton back. Circa 1880, Pennsylvania, excellent condition. $1,200.00 – 1,500.00.

Bottom: Pickle Dish. African-American, provenance known. Cotton. Hand pieced, hand quilted. Quilting: Baptist Fan. Cotton batt. Back brought around to front edge finish. Green cotton back. Circa 1925, Georgia, 65" x 78", good, some fading in border. $900.00 – 1,100.00.

Top: Log Cabin Barn Raising on point. Cotton. Machine pieced, hand quilted. Quilting: to pattern, with chevron in borders. Cotton batt. White applied straight grain binding. Muslin back. Circa 1880, Pennsylvania, excellent condition. $1,000.00 – 1,200.00.

Bottom: Log Cabin Barn Raising on point. Cotton. Machine pieced, hand quilted. Quilting: allover grid. Cotton batt. Back brought to front with radius corners. Large polka dot print back. Circa 1880, Pennsylvania, 82" x 80", good condition, some staining from the marking of quilting pattern. $650.00 – 750.00.

A. Detail of back and binding

A

A

B

A

Top: Log Cabin Barn Raising on point. Cotton. Machine pieced, hand quilted. Quilting: to pattern throughout. Cotton batt. Gray print applied straight grain binding. Paisley print back. Circa 1920, Pennsylvania, 76" x 76", excellent condition. $800.00 – 1,000.00.

A. Detail
B. Detail of back

Bottom: Log Cabin Barn Raising on point. Cotton. Machine pieced, hand quilted. Quilting: to pattern in blocks, zigzag in border. Cotton batt. Front brought to back edge finish. Red back. Circa 1875, Pennsylvania, 75" x 75", excellent condition. $750.00 – 900.00.

A. Detail of corner

A

Top: Perkioman Valley Split Nine Patch. Cotton. Machine pieced, hand quilted. Quilting: quadruple cable in border, 1" crosshatch on point, double parallel line along edge. Cotton batt. Front brought around to back and hand whipstitched. Muslin back. Circa 1920, Pennsylvania, 77" x 77", excellent condition. $900.00 – 1,100.00.
A. Detail of border and corner

Bottom: Mosaic #17 with values arranged in diagonal pattern. Cotton. Hand pieced, hand quilted. Quilting: to pattern and grid on point in border. Cotton batt. Back is brought to front edge finish. Blue print back. Circa 1890, Pennsylvania, 70" x 70", excellent condition. $900.00 – 1,200.00.
A. Detail of corner

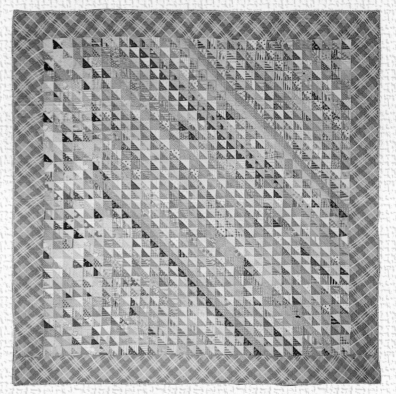

A

A

Basket center medallion. Unusual combination of elements. Cotton. Hand appliquéd, hand pieced, hand quilted. Quilting: interlocking circles throughout. Cotton batt. Back brought to front edge finish. Gray print back. Circa 1880, Pennsylvania, 77" x 80", excellent condition. $900.00 – 1,200.00.
A. Detail of center medallion

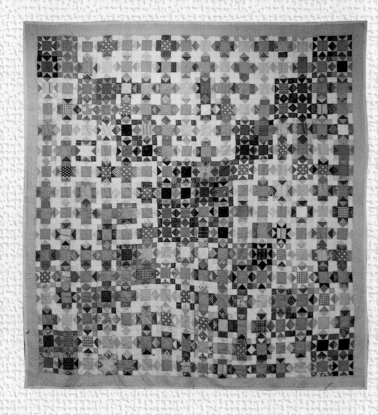

A

Sawtooth Star center medallion. Cotton. Hand and machine pieced, hand quilted. Quilting: to pattern, cable in border. Cotton batt. Back is brought to front edge finish. Pale blue/green flannel back. Circa 1890 blocks; finished circa 1940, Pennsylvania, 93" x 96", excellent condition. $950.00 – 1,050.00.
A. Detail of center medallion

A

B

Top: Original pieced design. Cotton. Machine pieced, hand quilted. Excellent quilting: allover grid, zigzag in border. Cotton batt. Front is brought to back edge finish. Muslin back. Circa 1920, Pennsylvania, 76" x 78", excellent condition, not accurately pieced. $500.00 – 750.00.
A. Detail of center
B. Detail of border

Bottom: Four Patch. Cotton. Hand pieced, hand quilted. Quilting: large overlapping circles. Cotton batt. Back brought to front edge finish. Small needlepoint print back. Circa 1875, Pennsylvania, 80" x 82", excellent condition. $350.00 – 500.00.
A. Detail of corner and border
B. Detail of back

A

B

A

Sampler quilt. Two sided. Cotton. Hand and machine pieced, poorly hand quilted. Quilting: 3" diagonal grid. Cotton batt. Knife edge. Pieced sampler back. Circa 1950, Midwest, 63" x 66", good condition, one small hole, slight fading, not accurately pieced. $600.00 – 750.00.

A. Back of quilt

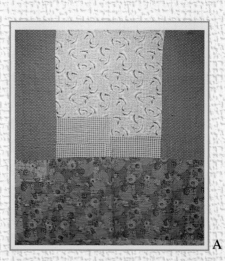

A

Three Block center medallion with multiple borders. Cotton. Hand and machine pieced, hand quilted. Quilting: ¼" inside of each seam throughout on front. Flannel fill. Knife edge finish. Back pieced from feed sacks. Circa 1950, Pennsylvania, 70" x 72", excellent condition. $400.00 – 500.00.

A. Back of quilt

A

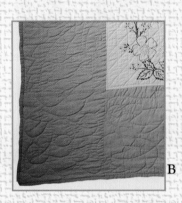

B

Top: Embroidered Flowers.
Cotton sateen. Machine pieced, hand embroidered, hand quilted. Quilting: floral, feather wreath, diagonal grid in blocks. Cotton batt. Green applied straight grain binding. Green back. Circa 1940, New England, 68" x 90", excellent condition. $600.00 – 750.00.
A. Detail
B. Detail of border

Bottom: Purple and white Baskets. Polished cotton. Machine pieced, heavily hand quilted. Quilting: feather motifs, floral, grid, to pattern. Cotton batt. Purple straight grain applied binding. White polished cotton. Circa 1940, New England, 84" x 86", excellent condition. $750.00 – 850.00.
A. Detail
B. Detail of quilting

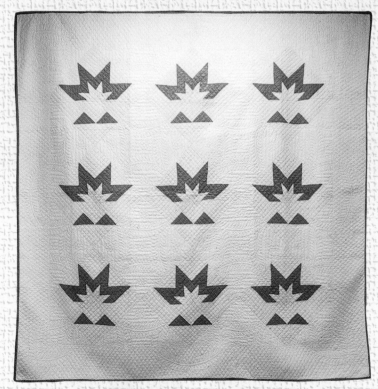

B

A

A

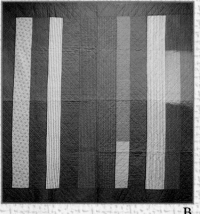

B

A

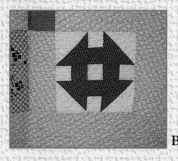

B

Top: Ohio Star variation. Cotton. Machine pieced, hand quilted. Quilting: crosshatch on point throughout. Cotton batt. Front brought to back edge finish. Pieced bars in a frame back. Circa 1900, Pennsylvania, 80" x 82½", fair condition due to fading on back and one edge. $400.00 – 600.00.
A. Detail of blocks
B. Detail of back

Bottom: Churn Dash. Cotton. Machine pieced, heavily hand quilted. Quilting: pumpkin seed in posts, cable in sashing, and grid in blocks. Cotton batt. Back brought to front binding. Muslin back. Circa 1920, New England, 74" x 74", excellent condition. $650.00.
A. Detail of blocks
B. Detail of corner

A

A

B

Top: Nine Patch on point.
Cotton. Hand pieced, hand quilted. Quilting: grid throughout. Cotton batt. Front brought to back edge finish. Blue and white woven plaid back. Circa 1910, Diehl family, Adams County, Pennsylvania, 78" x 80", excellent condition. $500.00 – 700.00.
A. Detail
B. Detail of back

Bottom: Streak of Lightening.
Cotton. Machine pieced, hand quilted in allover fan pattern. Cotton batting. Front brought to back edge finish. Back in muslin. Circa 1950, Midwest, 64" x 74", excellent condition. $600.00 – 675.00.
A. Detail

A

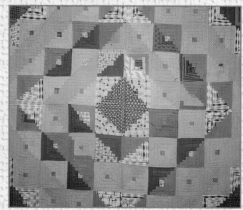

A

A

Top: Log Cabin Barn Raising. Wool challis. Foundation pieced quilt as you go method, hand pieced, hand quilted. Quilting: to pattern, diagonal grid on border. No batt. Blue applied straight grain binding. Checked fabrics pieced in bars back. Circa 1860, Pennsylvania, 82" x 82", excellent condition. $1,600.00 – 1,800.00.

 A. Detail of center

Bottom: Log Cabin Barn Raising with striped borders on three sides. Wool. Hand pieced, hand quilted. Quilting: to pattern. No batt. Black wool applied straight grain binding. Black back. Circa 1890, Pennsylvania, 69"x 73", excellent condition. $700.00 – 900.00.

 A. Detail of center

Top left: Amish Nine Patch on point. Wool. Hand pieced, hand quilted. Quilting: crosshatch, to pattern. Cotton batt. Front brought to back edge finish. Gray wool back. Circa 1910, Mifflin County, Pennsylvania, 68" x 72", excellent condition. $1,200.00 – 1,500.00.

Top right: Amish One Patch. Wool. Hand pieced, hand quilted. Quilting: to pattern, grid. Cotton batt. Gray applied wool straight grain binding. Burgundy wool back. Circa 1920, Mifflin County, Pennsylvania, 64" x 84", excellent condition. $900.00 – 1,200.00.

Bottom: Amish Lightning Streak. Wool. Machine pieced, hand quilted. Quilting: fan pattern throughout. Cotton batt. Dark brown wool bias applied binding. Black wool back. Circa 1890, Missouri, 63" x 78", poor condition. $300.00 – 400.00.

A. Detail
B. Detail

A

B

A

B

Top left: Amish Framed Rectangles. Wool. Machine pieced, hand quilted. Quilting: parallel lines throughout. Quilted in black thread. Cotton batt. Front brought to back edge finish. Lavender cotton back. Circa 1930, Mifflin County, Pennsylvania, 65" x 82", poor condition, moth holes. $300.00 – 400.00.

Top right: Mennonite Roman Stripe or Basket Weave. Wool and silk. Machine pieced, hand embroidered, hand quilted. Quilting: to pattern, cable in border. Cotton batt. Front brought to back edge finish. Striped flannel back. Circa 1900, Pennsylvania, 80" x 80", excellent condition. $900.00 – 1,200.00.

Bottom: Mennonite Hearts and Gizzards. Wool. Machine pieced, hand embroidered, hand quilted. Quilting: Chevron, to pattern. Cotton batt. Black applied wool bias binding. Orange and green striped flannel back. Circa 1920, Pennsylvania, 76" x 76", excellent condition. $600.00 – 700.00.

A. Detail of corner
B. Detail of back

A. B.

Top left: Pieced diamonds in Tumbling Blocks or Star in Hexagon formation. Wool. Machine pieced, hand quilted. Quilting: to pattern throughout. Cotton batt. Back is brought to front edge finish. Blue flannel back. Circa 1930, Pennsylvania, 72" x 79", excellent condition. $500.00 – 700.00.

Top right: Double Rows of Four Patches set in Bars hap. Wool. Machine pieced, hand embroidered, hand quilted. Quilting: grid and point in borders and parallel lines. Quilted in blue thread. Embroidered in blue and red decorative stitches on seams. Cotton batt. Knife edge with embroidery on edge. Striped flannel back. Circa 1910, Pennsylvania, 60" x 79", excellent condition. $800.00 – 1,000.00.
A. Detail
B. Detail

Bottom: Nine Patch hap. Wool. Machine pieced, hand quilted. Quilting: large diagonal crosshatch. Cotton batt. Applied straight grain binding. Striped flannel back. Circa 1900, Pennsylvania, 60" x 79", excellent condition. $500.00 – 700.00.

A

C

B

Top: One Patch center medallion hap. Wool. Machine pieced, hand quilted. Quilting: large grid throughout. Cotton batt. Knife edge. Fine cotton sateen green floral print. Circa 1920, Pennsylvania, 69" x 80", excellent condition. $350.00 – 450.00.
A. Detail of center
B. Detail of back
C. Detail of corner

Bottom: Pieced abstract design. Wool. Machine pieced, hand quilted. Quilting: straight line and 45 degree angles. Cotton batt. Back brought to front edge finish. Circa 1900, Missouri, 60" x 79", good condition. $800.00 – 1,000.00.

Top: Lone Stars with Stars in corners. Wool. Machine pieced, hand quilted. Quilting: Baptist Fans throughout. Cotton batt. Back to front edge finish. Green striped flannel back. Circa 1910, Pennsylvania, 75" x 75", excellent condition. $450.00 – 550.00.

Bottom: Center medallion with crazy patches. Each seam is embroidered. Wool. Machine pieced, hand embroidered, hand quilted. Quilting: large overall grid in pink thread. Blanket fill. Back to front edge finish. Raspberry cotton back. Circa 1920, Pennsylvania, 76" x 78", excellent condition. $650.00 – 800.00.
A. Detail of center
B. Detail of back

A

B

47

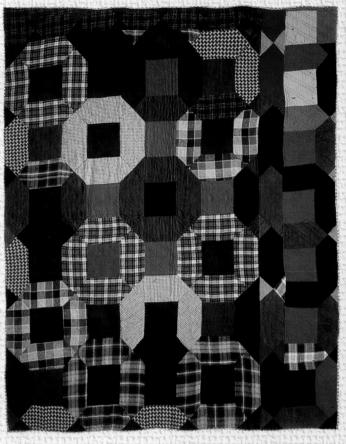

Top left: Embroidered crazy quilt. Wool. Machine pieced, hand embroidered, hand quilted. Quilting: around each block. Flannel sheet batt. Blue applied straight grain binding. Blue cotton sateen back. Circa 1910, Pennsylvania, 70" x 84", excellent condition. $800.00 – 900.00.

Top right: Kansas Dugout variation. Wool. Machine pieced, hand quilted. Quilting: parallel straight line. Cotton batt. Back is brought to front edge finish. Printed floral and geometric back. Circa 1930, Iowa, 71" x 89", excellent condition. $500.00 – 700.00.

Bottom: Spiderweb. Wool and velvet. Hand pieced, hand quilted. Quilting: zigzag, straight parallel lines, grid in center, in the ditch. Cotton batt. Back brought to front edge finish. Circa 1910, Pennsylvania, 76" x 76". $700.00 – 900.00.

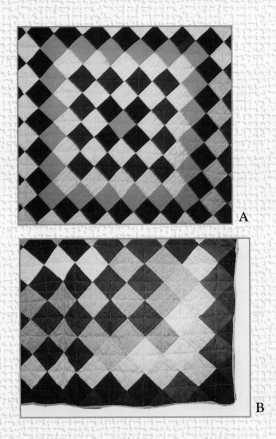

A

B

A

Top: Trip Around the World on point. Wool. Machine pieced, hand quilted. Quilting: horizontal and vertical lines through each square. Cotton batt. Salmon applied wool straight grain binding. Gray flannel back. Circa 1910, Pennsylvania, 77" x 80", excellent condition. $500.00 – 650.00.
A. Detail of center
B. Detail of edge

Bottom: Center medallion with pieced frames. Wool. Machine pieced, hand quilted. Quilting: Baptist Fans throughout. Cotton batt. Back to front edge finish. Blue chambray back. Circa 1915, Missouri, 65" x 80", fair condition. $350.00 – 500.00.
A. Detail of center

A

B

Trip Around the World.
Wool. Machine pieced, hand quilted. Quilting: allover grid on point using big red stitches. Cotton batt. Back brought to front edge finish. Blue striped flannel back. Circa 1920, Pennsylvania, 70" x 80", excellent condition. $400.00 – 600.00.

A. Detail of center
B. Detail

Doll and Crib Quilts

Crib and doll quilts are particularly fascinating and appealing to collectors. Not just because they are easily exhibited, stored, and cared for, but also because of their rarity — crib quilts were made for children so therefore, rare because they would have been subject to washing and wear; doll quilts, usually made by children for their dolls, were subjected to a similar amount of wear.

Both crib and doll quilts are desirable especially when these criteria are met:
Excellent condition: Very seldom is one found in excellent or unused condition. If so, then it will be reflected in the price.
Scaled down version of a full-size quilt. Block size is reduced in scale, while the pattern is repeated as in a full-size quilt.
Borders are present.
Quality of workmanship — piecing, appliqué, and quilting
Visual appeal
Rarity of design

Because these types of quilts are so desirable and expensive, an occasional "forgery" may surface in the marketplace. An important factor when purchasing either a crib or doll quilt is to determine if it is right or not. By "right," we mean authentic and not reproduced or cut down from a full-size quilt. Be very careful to examine the edge binding, etc. to ascertain originality.

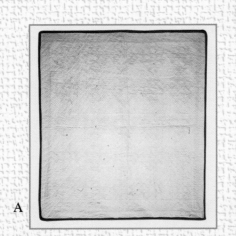

A

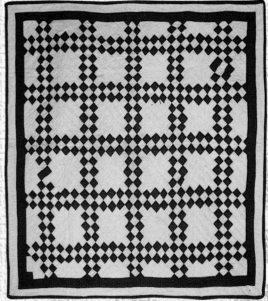

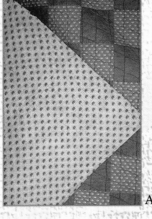

A

Top: Blue and white Irish Chain crib quilt. Cotton. Hand pieced, hand quilted, hand appliquéd. Quilting: to pattern, diagonal grid. Cotton batt. Blue applied straight grain binding. Muslin back. Circa 1885, New England, 36" x 39", excellent condition. $600.00 – 750.00.

A. Detail of back

Bottom: Red and green Checkerboard crib quilt. No borders. Simple pattern – not scaled down. Cotton. Hand pieced, hand quilted. Quilting: 2" diamonds throughout. Cotton batt. Back brought to front edge finish. Print back. Circa 1860, Pennsylvania, 41" x 43", excellent condition. $350.00 – 500.00.

A. Detail of back

A.

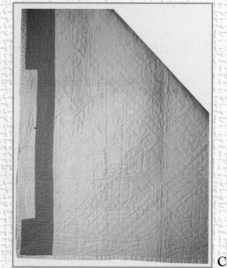

B.

C.

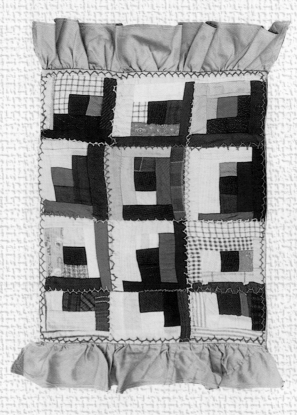

Top: Pink and green Bear's Paw crib quilt. Cotton. Machine pieced, hand quilted. Quilting: to pattern, pumpkin seed, diagonal grid, cable. Cotton batt. Knife edge. Red pieced back. Circa 1880, Pennsylvania, 39" x 46", excellent condition. $400.00 – 600.00.

    A. Detail of block
    B. Detail of corner
    C. Detail of back

Bottom: Log Cabin doll quilt with ruffle border. Wool, cotton, flannel, and voile. Hand pieced, hand embroidered. No quilting. No batt. Ruffle on top and bottom edges, knife edge finish on sides. Green cotton sateen back. Circa 1900, 13½" x 15¾" plus 3½" ruffle at top and bottom, very good condition. $250.00 – 350.00.

A

B

Top: Yellow and red Checkerboard crib quilt with red print border. Cotton. Machine pieced, hand quilted. Quilting: 1½" grid on point. Cotton batt. Front brought around to back edge finish. Pieced red and green bars on back. Circa 1880, Pennsylvania, 42" x 43½", excellent condition. $450.00 – 600.00.
A. Detail of corner
B. Detail of back

Bottom: Dresden Plate crib quilt. Cotton. Hand pieced, hand appliquéd, hand quilted. Excellent quilting: Feather wreath, ¼" to pattern, parallel diagonal lines, pumpkin seeds. Cotton batt. Applied straight grain binding. White cotton back. Circa 1930, 50" x 50", excellent condition. $550.00 – 700.00.
A. Detail of block

A

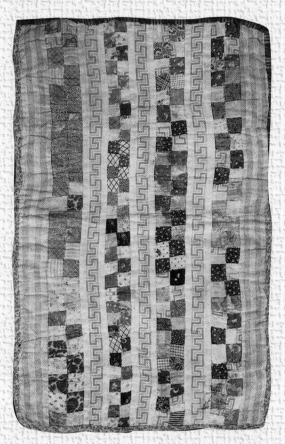

A

B

Top: Four Patch strippy doll quilt. Cotton. Hand pieced, hand quilted. Quilting: large grid pattern. Cotton batt. Blue plaid hand applied straight grain binding. Brown print back. Circa 1875, New England, 12½" x 19", fair/good condition, some soil and stains. $300.00 – 450.00.

A. Detail of front
B. Detail of back

Bottom: Redwork squirrel doll quilt. Cotton. Hand embroidered. Flannel fill. Red applied straight grain binding. White back. Circa 1910, 17" x 24½", excellent condition. $200.00.

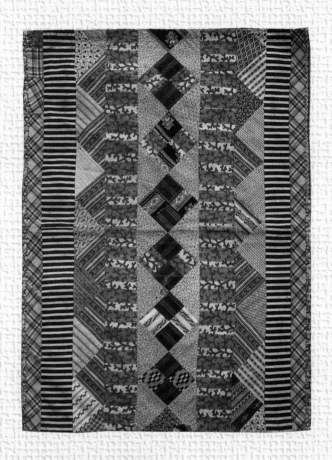

A

B

Four Patch strippy doll quilt with early Madder prints. Cotton. Hand pieced, hand quilted. Quilting: vertical rows. No batt. Sides have applied straight grain binding; top and bottom have faced edge finish. Back is brown muslin from fugitive dyes. Circa 1840, New England, 16½" x 23", fair/good condition, a few worn areas. $500.00 – 650.00.
A. Detail of front
B. Detail of back

55

Whole Cloth Bedcovers
British, French, and American

Joseph Marie Jacquard (1782 – 1834) invented the Jacquard loom in France in 1804. About 1820 or as soon as weavers became sophisticated in their operation of the Jacquard loom and thereby, perfecting the process for weaving large bedcovers, weavings of this style of textile began. White work bedcovers or quilts done in Italy and France by hand were now being produced by this method, which resulted in the same sort of effects as the handmade pieces. These intricately designed bed coverings were very decorative and highly sought after by the European, English, and American markets. These looms were capable of producing and supplying the demand more readily, easily, and therefore, cheaply. Production expanded to other countries including America, where the trend continued through the late 1800s.

The French began exporting textiles from this industry through the Port of Marseilles, which was the biggest port in France in the eighteenth century. These bedcovers originated in Provence, but became known as Marseille spreads, where they were shipped from rather than where they were made.

By the mid to late nineteenth century, America was producing them also and continues today because their popularity continues. They became especially popular after the Victorian period as a reaction against the dark, busy styles of that era. The more pronounced or puffy the design, the better, which tends to describe the earlier examples.

The handmade bride's quilt from the late nineteenth to early twentieth century was also popular. The reason for their popularity would also be reaction to the Victorian styles. This, coupled with the expense of purchasing Marseille spreads would perhaps be the reason white on white handmade quilts became so much a part of a girl's wedding preparations.

Today, these white quilts and spreads are especially sought after by decorators to supply current trends and demands. White is a very popular color for home décor. The elegant look of these bedcovers with their intricate raised designs is especially desirable. Condition is important; stains and wear considerably affect their price.

A

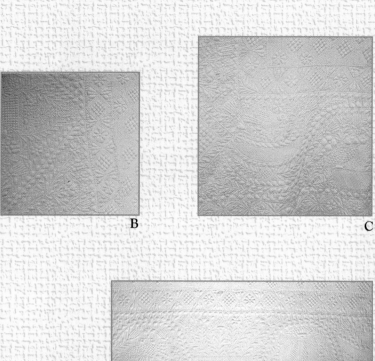

B

C

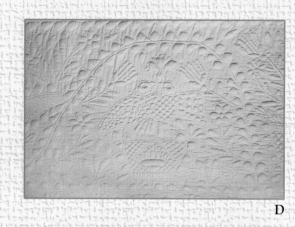

D

E

F

G

H

Broderie de Marseille. Provence, France. White cotton Wedding quilt. Hand stitched. Heavily stuffed and corded. Knife edge finish. Late eighteenth – early nineteenth century, 93" x 103", very good condition. Originally in the collection of Electra Havemeyer Webb, Shelburne, Vermont. $20,000.00.

A. Detail
B. Detail
C. Detail
D. Detail
E. Detail
F. Detail
G. Detail
H. Detail
I. Detail
J. Detail

I

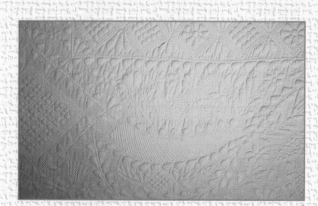

J

A

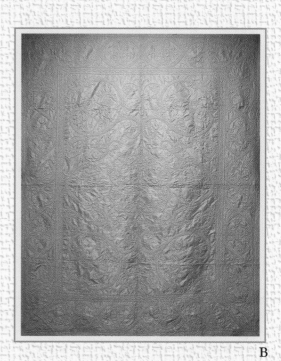

B

C

D

Boutis. France. Silk. Reversible. Corded and stuffed bedcover. Gold silk/peach silk. Corded knife edge finish. Late eighteenth – early nineteenth century, 70" x 86", very good condition. $4,000.00 – 6,000.00.

A. Detail of gold side
B. Full view peach side
C. Detail peach side
D. Detail peach side

Top: Boutis. White cotton reversible. Small (crib) bedcover. Stuffed and corded. Heavily quilted. Quilting: center double diagonal grid, cable, and straight parallel lines along edges. Corded knife edge finish. Initialed in red: "L.B." in one corner. Excellent condition. $600.00 – 800.00.
A. Detail of corner
B. Detail of initials

Bottom: Bolton coverlet. English. Initialed and dated, "SSF 1812." Design looks similar to Candlewick. One piece. Eight-pointed Star center medallion with a series of borders – swag, trees, flowers, etc. Cotton. 92" x 106", excellent condition. $4,000.00 – 6,000.00.
A. Detail
B. Detail
C. Detail of corner

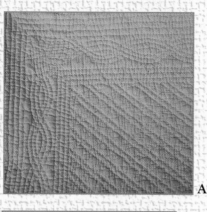

A

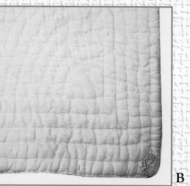

B

A

B

C

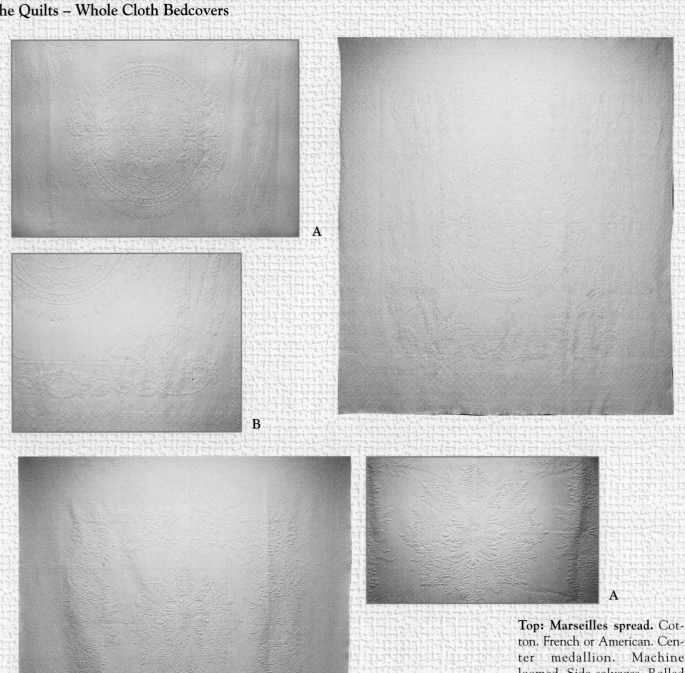

A

B

A

Top: Marseilles spread. Cotton. French or American. Center medallion. Machine loomed. Side selvages. Rolled edge hand-finished top and bottom. Circa 1880, 74" x 82", excellent condition. $350.00 – 500.00.

A. Detail
B. Detail of corner

Bottom: Marseilles spread. Cotton. French or American. Center medallion. Machine loomed. Two side selvages. Machine hemmed top and bottom. Circa 1880, 80" x 80", excellent condition. $350.00 – 550.00.

A. Detail of center
B. Detail of corner

B

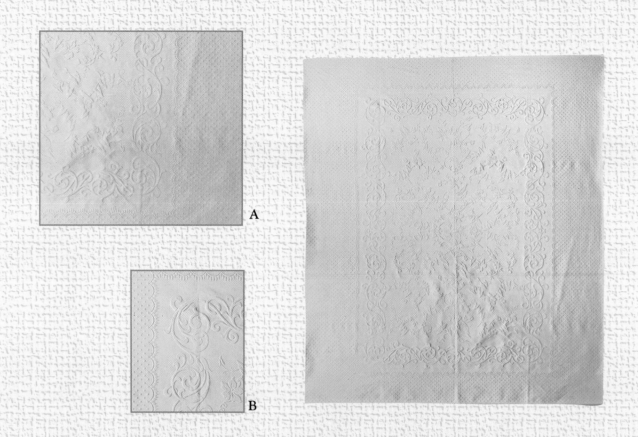

A

B

A

B

Top: Marseilles spread. Cotton. French or American. Allover design. Polka-dot border. Two side selvages. Top and bottom hand hemmed. Machine woven. Circa 1890, 74" x 82", excellent condition. $300.00 – 450.00.
A. Detail
B. Detail

Bottom: Bride's quilt. White on white whole cloth center medallion. Hand quilted: grid on point, very complex feather wreath, cable and floral border. Cotton batting. Applied bias binding. White back. Circa 1890, Pennsylvania, 75" x 80", excellent condition. $600.00 – 700.00.
A. Detail
B. Detail

A

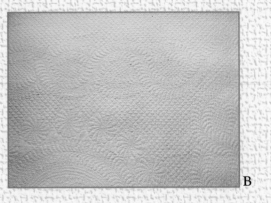

B

Bride's quilt. White on white whole cloth center medallion. Hand quilted: grid on point as fill for a very complex center medallion surrounded by small circular patterns and feathered scrolls going into the corners. Cotton batting. Applied straight binding. White back. Circa 1890, Pennsylvania, 76" x 76", excellent condition. $650.00 – 750.00.

A. Detail
B. Detail

Pillow Covers

Shams, cases, covers, and toppers are some of the terms used to describe covers for pillows and bolsters. One of the rarest examples of bed furnishings are pieced and appliquéd pillow and bolster covers. Those that have survived are in unused condition, which indicates they were highly prized and strictly decorative.

Very few examples exist outside of the New York, New Jersey, and Pennsylvania area so it would appear to be a regional style with Dutch and German roots. Their rarity contributes to their value. When they appear for sale, there is an eager market willing to pay high prices. Generally, the more skill that was required to execute the technique used or the complexity of design increases the desirability.

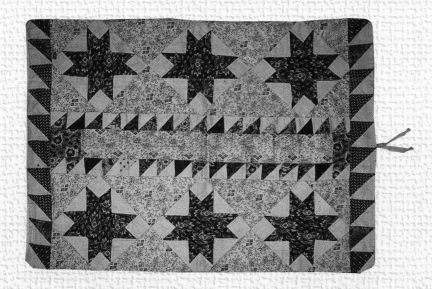

A

C

B

Pieced Evening Stars with Sawtooth edges. Cotton. Hand pieced. Muslin back. Lined with brown printed fabric behind patchwork. Woven twill tape ties sewn inside to contain pillow. Circa 1840, New York, 18" x 25", very rare. $500.00 – 600.00, one only.
A. Detail
B. Detail
C. Detail

Pillow Covers

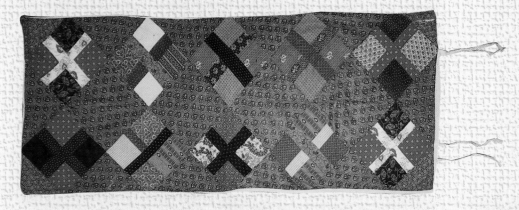

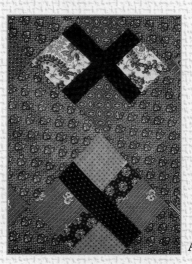

A

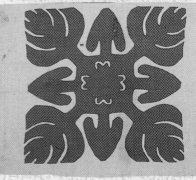

A

Top: Pieced bolster cover
Cotton. Hand pieced
Crossed Four Patch with tie
– ⅜" twill tape at open end
Muslin back. Never used
Circa 1840, Pennsylvania
19" x 49". $600.00 – 750.00
one only.

A. Detai

**Bottom: Pair of Pennsylva
nia Dutch appliquéd pillow
cases.** Cotton. Hand
appliquéd and reverse
appliquéd. Back is the same
tiny blue and white print a
front. Never used. Circa
1860, Pennsylvania, 18" x
25½". $450.00 – 600.00 pair.

A. Detai

64

A

B

Top: Pair of Pennsylvania Dutch appliquéd pillow cases with two appliqué patterns. Cotton. Hand appliquéd and reverse appliquéd. Muslin back. Never used. Circa 1875, Pennsylvania, 17" x 35". $500.00 – 700.00 pair.
A. Detail
B. Detail

Bottom: Pair of Pennsylvania Dutch Tulip Wreath appliqué with appliquéd border as open end. Cotton. Hand appliquéd. Tiny black dot fabric front and back. Never used. Circa 1875, Pennsylvania, 17" x 35". $450.00 – 600.00 pair.
A. Detail

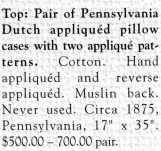

A

Pillow Covers

A

B

A

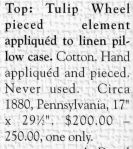

C

Top: Tulip Wheel pieced element appliquéd to linen pillow case. Cotton. Hand appliquéd and pieced. Never used. Circa 1880, Pennsylvania, 17" x 29½". $200.00 – 250.00, one only.

A. Detail

Bottom: Pair Nine Patch on point with Sawtooth borders. Cotton. Machine pieced. Same blue print fabric on back. Never used. Circa 1880, Pennsylvania, 18½" x 29½". $325.00 – 375.00 pair.

A. Detail of back
B. Detail
C. Detail

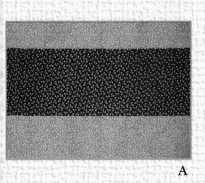

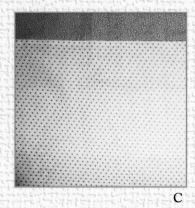

A

B

C

Top: Pair Bars pillow cases. Cotton. Machine pieced. Simple horizontal bars pattern of red and green. Blue and white print back. Never used. Circa 1880, Pennsylvania, 18¾" x 30½". $250.00 – 350.00 pair.
A. Detail
B. Detail
C. Detail

Bottom: Whole cloth printed bolster cover. Cotton. Muslin back. Never used. Circa 1860, New England, 19" x 35". $150.00 – 250.00, one only.

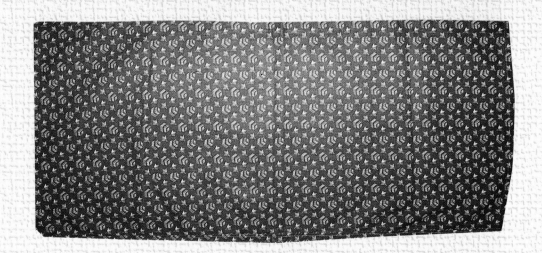

Pillow Covers

Top: Pair of homespun pillow covers. Homespun cotton. Red and white plaid with hand embroidered chain stitch decorative designs. Homespun cotton back. Never used. Circa 1840, New Jersey, 17" x 36". $400.00 – 600.00 pair.

A. Detail
B. Detail

Bottom: Crazy patch pillow cover. Wool, cotton, and cotton flannel. Pieced and embroidered. Gray cotton back. Dated in embroidery Jan. 1912, Midwest, 13" x 15". excellent condition. $75.00 – 125.00, one only.

A. Detail

A

B

A

Quilt Tops and Summer Spreads

We refer to quilt tops, pieced, appliquéd, or a combination, that were left unquilted, as tops. They exist for various reasons. Producing tops was much more popular than quilting and faster so it stands to reason they would accumulate more rapidly than quilted examples. Piecing and appliqué were much more fun for a majority of quiltmakers because they represent the more creative aspect of the craft.

Quilt history has become a popular subject for historians and researchers, especially interested in women's studies. As a result, quilts, tops, blocks, and fabrics relating to quiltmaking have become popular. Collectors have always had an interest, so the market has broadened.

Tops provide an opportunity to examine the work from the back providing different kinds of information than just from the front. They also show the top and fabrics as they were when the top was created, unlike quilts which were subjected to wear, fading, and the abuse of everyday use.

Over time, they have become increasingly desirable among collectors and historians. They are smaller and therefore, easier to store, but still represent the history and fabrics of the times. As a result of their popularity, prices have escalated. Today, an interesting top can fetch what a quilt used to bring. Age, rarity of pattern, and condition all play important roles in buying wisely. A top should be in unwashed condition as washing can affect quality. Seam allowances can be compromised when a top is washed. The washing can unravel the fabric to the point where it will fall apart. Without the protection of quilting, many pieced tops will suffer from washing.

Often future generations would finish them but not in their intended form. Quilting skills diminished with time and demands. Women often were not able or interested in learning or pursuing quilting as a pastime activity. As a result, these tops were often just backed, bound, and tied to prepare them for use. Occasionally, the edges were finished without backing. They would not have the warmth of a quilt so were often used as cover in the summer — thus the term summer spread. Because these items were not used for warmth, they often survived in good condition. Usually costing less than quilts while still visually exciting and much easier to store, collectors have become increasingly more interested in summer spreads.

As in all areas of collecting, condition, rarity, workmanship, and age contribute to the value.

Quilt Tops

A

Court House Lawn. Cotton. Machine pieced. Circa 1900, Pennsylvania, 64" x 64", excellent condition. $350.00.

A. Detail of block

Quilt Tops and Summer Spreads

Top left: **Sawtooth medallion.** Cotton. Machine pieced. Circa 1930, New England, 64" x 76", excellent condition. $275.00.

Top right: **Bear's Paw.** Cotton. Machine pieced. Circa 1875, Pennsylvania, 60" x 63", excellent condition. $225.00.

Bottom: **Wild Goose Chase.** Cotton. Machine pieced. Circa 1880, 74" x 77", excellent condition. $300.00.

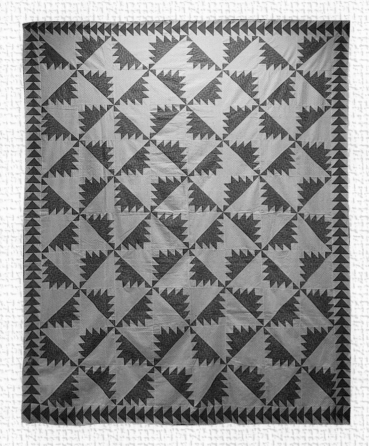

A

A

Top: Kansas Troubles with Wild Goose Chase border. Cotton. Machine pieced. Circa 1900, New England, 73" x 92", excellent condition. $350.00.
A. Detail of block

Bottom: String Diamonds in Bars setting. Cotton. Machine pieced. Circa 1890, Pennsylvania, 80" x 80", excellent condition. $275.00.
A. Detail

A

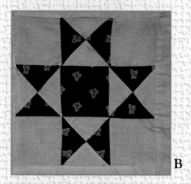

B

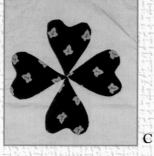

C

Top: Eight-Pointed Star with Hex, Heart, and Diamond setting. Cotton. Hand pieced. Circa 1840, Pennsylvania, 54" x 72", excellent condition. $350.00.

A. Detail
B. Detail
C. Detail

Bottom: True Lover's Knot. Cotton. Machine pieced. Circa 1890, New England, 82" x 82", excellent condition. $400.00.

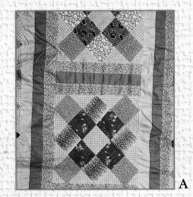

A

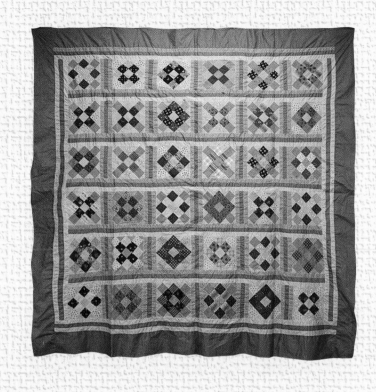

B

A

Top: Lattice and Square.
Cotton. Machine pieced.
Circa 1920, Pennsylvania,
80" x 80", excellent condition. $275.00.
A. Detail
B. Detail

Bottom: House. Cotton.
Machine pieced. Circa 1910,
Upstate New York, 60" x 80",
excellent condition. $800.00.
A. Detail

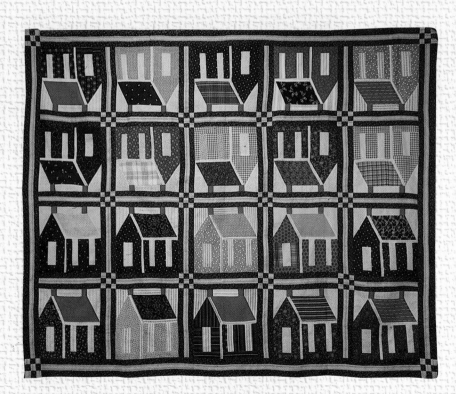

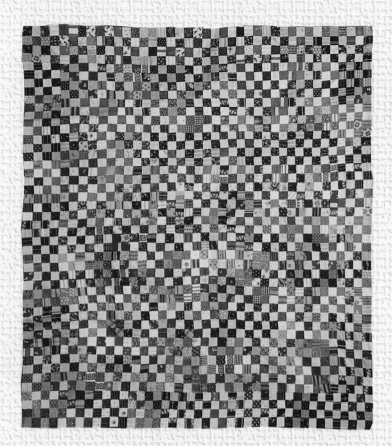

A

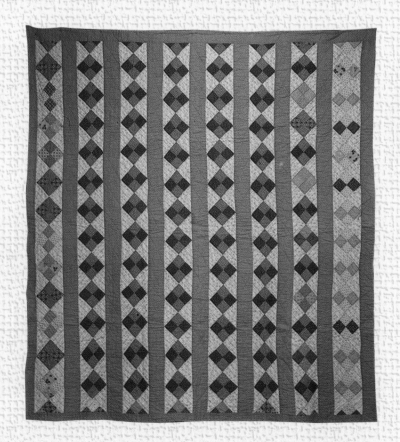

Top: Four Patch Postage Stamp. Cotton. Machine pieced. 1¼" squares. Circa 1890, Pennsylvania, 52" x 58", excellent condition. $395.00.

A. Detail

Bottom: Four Patch on point in bars. Cotton. Machine pieced. Circa 1880, 70" x 76", excellent condition. $350.00.

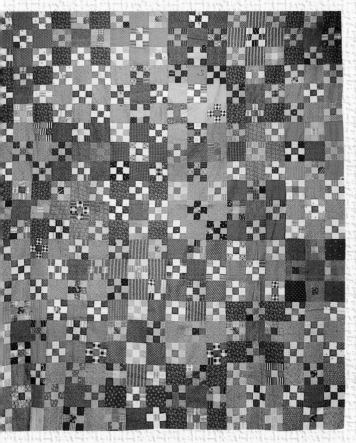

Top left: Nine Patch. Cotton. Machine pieced. Circa 1890, Pennsylvania, 68" x 68", excellent condition. $275.00.

Top right: Sampler. Cotton. Machine and hand pieced. Circa 1880, Pennsylvania, 86" x 92", excellent condition. $395.00.

Bottom: Broken Dishes. Cotton. Machine pieced. Circa 1890, Pennsylvania, 80" x 80", excellent condition. $250.00.
A. Detail

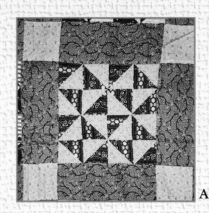

A

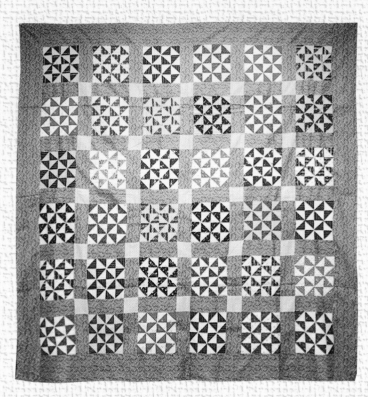

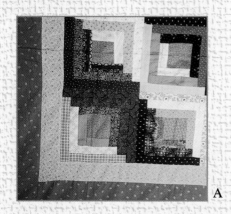

A

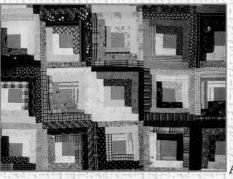

A

Top: Log Cabin Barn Raising on point. Cotton. Machine pieced. Circa 1890, Berks County, Pennsylvania, 80" x 80", excellent condition. $350.00.

A. Detail

Bottom: Log Cabin Barn Raising (no borders). Machine pieced. Circa 1880, Pennsylvania, 65" x 66⅛". $200.00.

A. Detail

A

A

Top: Log Cabin Dark and Light. Machine pieced. Circa 1890, Pennsylvania, 78" x 78". $250.00.
A. Detail

Bottom: Touching Stars. Hand-pieced blocks, machine assembled. Circa 1890, Pennsylvania, 79" x 80". $350.00.
A. Detail of corner

Quilt Tops and Summer Spreads

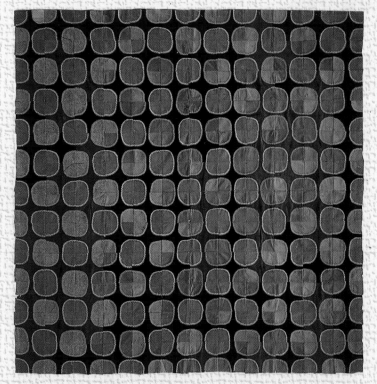

Top left: Log Cabin Straight Furrow. Cotton. Machine pieced. Circa 1910, Pennsylvania, 72" x 72", excellent condition. $325.00.

Top right: Basket Weave. Cotton. Machine pieced. Circa 1890, Pennsylvania, 80" x 80", excellent condition. $325.00.

Bottom: Snowball. Wool. Hand appliquéd, hand embroidered. Circa 1900, Michigan, 67" x 67", excellent condition. $400.00.

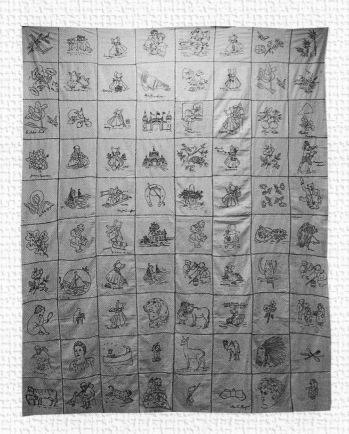

A

Top: Redwork days of the week, months, and seasons with signatures. Cotton. Hand embroidered, machine pieced. Circa 1900, New York, 64" x 84", excellent condition. $295.00.
A. Detail

Bottom: Dresden Plate. Cotton. Hand pieced, hand appliquéd. Circa 1930, Illinois, 70" x 80", excellent condition. $225.00.

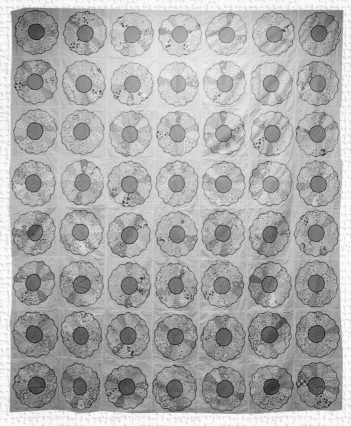

Summer Spreads

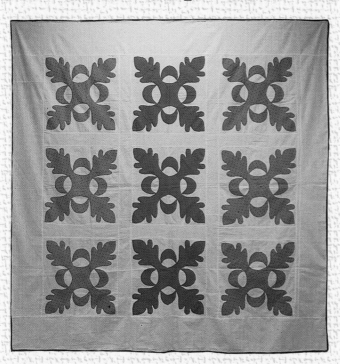

Top: Oak Leaf and Reel. Cotton. Hand appliquéd, machine pieced. Red appliec bias binding. Top circa 1880 bound circa 1940, 76" x 78" excellent condition. $500.00.
A. Detai

Bottom: Star of Bethlehem with Stars in corners. Cotton. Hand pieced and appliquéd. Front brought to back. Circa 1860, 75½" x 75½ excellent condition, Osborne H. Abbott family. $600.00 – 750.00.

A. Detail
B. Detail

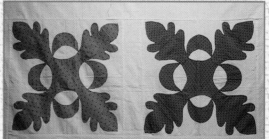

A

A

B

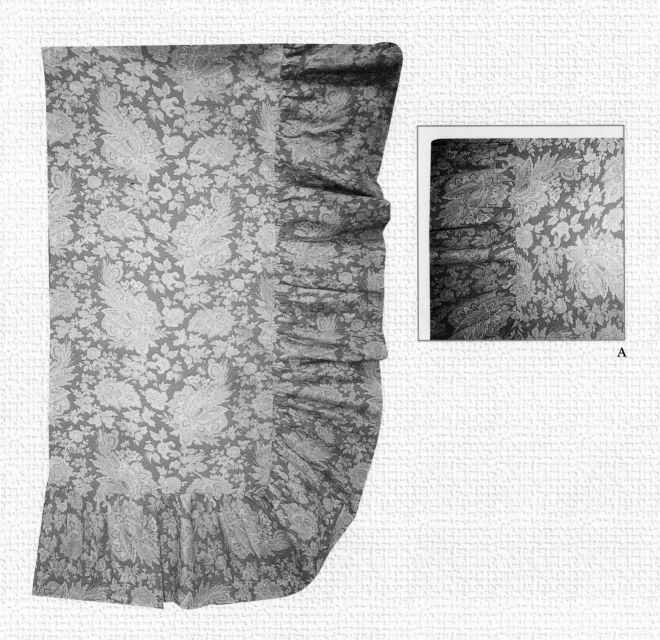

A

Duvet (comforter cover). Large cotton floral print. Machine constructed. Tiny print (red) cotton lining. 11" ruffle on three sides. Circa 1880, New England, 48" x 80", excellent condition. $250.00.
A. Detail

A

B

C

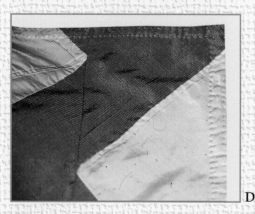

D

E

Center medallion silk bed-cover. Pieced and appliquéd with silk thread. Broderie perse, hand pieced, appliquéd, and embellished with metallic thread, embroidery, and steel sequins. Knife edge finish, stitched with two rows, ¼" apart, running stitch at the very edge. Hand seamed silk back. Circa 1790 – 1810, English, 82" x 85", excellent condition. $5,000.00.
A. Detail
B. Detail
C. Detail
D. Detail
E. Detail

Comforts

QUILT OR COMFORT?
1880 – 1930

Quilts are three layers connected by a running stitch visible top and back. Comforts, comforters, haps, counterpanes are not. It is difficult because these terms do not mean the same thing to everyone. Antique inventories of household goods list those items but it is uncertain as to what specifically is being mentioned. There are no physical descriptions to identify any of these items.

For our purposes, because many of these terms are regional, any bedcover quilted is a quilt. Anything tied is a comfort, except for a particular type of comfort coming from rural Pennsylvania called a hap which when tied is technically a comfort. Not all haps are tied. There are those that are quilted as well. They still fall into the same category however because they are very heavily stuffed, usually of wool or cotton. Tops are of very coarse materials, wool, etc. What appears to be common in all cases is a decorative embroidery stitch at the seams — a feature remaining from the Victorian era. When quilted because of the thickness, it is very crude with large stitches, and often backed with flannel.

A comfort is a top, middle layer of batting (wool or cotton) thicker and heavier than in a quilt and a back; just like a quilt. Because it is thick and heavy it is tied. A cord, yarn, or thread is drawn through all three layers brought back through all three layers at about an inch apart and tied at the top or back depending on preference. Sometimes, there is a decorative finishing on the top by fraying the ties or adding some detail. This serves to hold the three layers together when they are placed approximately 3" to 4" apart. Most often they are placed at junctures with regards to the design of the top. The ties can be an important element in the visual appeal. They add color, texture, and a three-dimensional quality that is very different from a quilt.

The top can be pieced like quilts but often these pieces are of coarser materials i.e. wool and, if pieced, they are simple in design: Four Patch, Irish Chain, other simple geometric designs or simple stars. The ties can also be of colored yarn and can provide another decorative element.

The edges are often simply finished by turning in the back and the front creating a knife edge. The edge is simply overcast or blanket stitched. There are other, more elaborate edge finishes. Some are fringed, ruffled, scalloped, have crocheted edges, or even felted wool pierced with designs and finished with a fancy decorative edge. As you might imagine, they are very heavy. They would provide warmth with one cover, rather than layers. They also were much faster to produce than quilts and could be taken apart easily to be cleaned. The ties were cut, the top and back either wet cleaned or dry cleaned, and it was reassembled, either with the same filling or new.

There are also those tied comforts that are made out of earlier tops that were never quilted during the time they were made. It is not difficult to understand how nineteenth century pieced tops were put into household use by later generations that inherited them. Not every household continued to carry on the tradition of quiltmaking. As women's responsibilities changed, which often included working outside the home, many time-consuming tasks were abandoned. Tying a top and finishing in this manner provided a useful bedcover without the investment of time that was no longer available.

World War I took many women out of the home and put them in factories or in business. A great amount of comforts come from the early twentieth century and many are late nineteenth century tops, made into comforts later.

The materials being courser wools, etc., give many of these pieces a very different appearance. Very often, woolen sample books were taken apart and used. These were rectangular and often you will see that shape repeatedly in comforts. The Victorian crazy patch is often used as well, natural for this style. As in everything, there are those that are more pleasing than others. One would expect it to be very difficult for a traditional quilter to abandon all the disciplined techniques of fine quiltmaking to participate in the making of comforts. It perhaps appealed to the generation making crazy quilts, where the skill level was different and accuracy was not such an issue. The appeal that these pieces have is not unlike that of a traditional quilt; however, they tend to be bold geometric designs or subtle dark blues, earth tones, and grays because of the use of wools, often the kind found in men's suits.

They can be very striking, dynamic, and energetic. Many have found their way into galleries, shops, collections, and museums. Today with interests going more toward the less formal, less traditional examples have created a market for comforts and therefore, the demand is greater and their values are increasing. Much of what you will see in this section is improvisational but it existed before improvisational was a word used to describe quilts.

Comforts

Comfort is a name given to those bedcovers that are tied rather than quilted. They are tied usually because the top is of heavy material, most often wool. They are stuffed or filled with thick cotton, wool, another quilt, or any combination of the above. They are tied because the thickness would be too great to penetrate with a needle and thread, using a running stitch. The ties are usually cotton, sometimes wool, or embroidery floss. They are most often tied at regular intervals connecting the three layers uniformly to prevent separation. The top very often determines the placement of the ties. The ties can be obvious on the top as an intended decoration; can be brought to the back hidden from the front or not obvious front or back.

Comforts or haps as they are known in a particular area in Pennsylvania (Oley Valley) characteristically are pieced tops similar to quilts with larger, fewer, and less intricate designs. The limited design possibilities created by the thickness of wool require the piecing to be simple. As a result, the designs can be strong, dynamic, contrasting, and exciting geometric arrangements. The color of wool being more saturated than cotton presents a visual experience quite different from that of cotton quilts. Wool rectangles from salesmen's wool sample books, recycled into bedcovers, was a good practical design source.

They occur late nineteenth century and well into the twentieth century. Carryover from the Victorian period, embroidery stitching occurs on those from the turn of the century to the 1920s. As quilting declined after 1900, quite often earlier cotton tops will appear finished in this manner. The backs on these comforts are most often flannel. The edges turned inward creating a knife edge treatment sometimes stitched along the edge with decorative stitching in addition to those necessary to complete the edge.

This type of bedcover is prevalent in every area where quilts are found. Perhaps the availability of wool from mill end outlets account for the popularity of wool comforts rather than cotton quilts.

A

B

C

Log Cabin multiple Barn Raising on point. Silk. Machine pieced, hand embroidered, hand tied in red. No batt. Knife edge with embroidery. Decorative embroidery stitches on every block seam. Commercial quilted red silk back. Circa 1890, Lebanon County, Pennsylvania, 62" x 62", excellent condition. $1,200.00.

A. Detail of center
B. Detail of edge
C. Detail of back

A

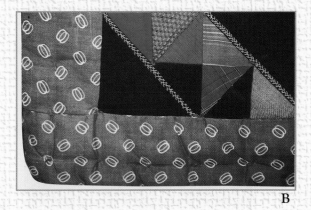

B

C

Barn Raising set with Pinwheel center hap. Wool and cotton. Hand pieced, hand embroidered, hand tied. Embroidery outlining solid dark areas. Cotton batt. Knife edge straight stitched edge finish. Brown checked wool back. Circa 1910, Pennsylvania, 66" x 66½", excellent condition. $700.00 – 900.00.

A. Detail of center
B. Detail of front corner
C. Detail of back

B

C

A

Trip Around the World on point. Wool. Machine pieced, hand tied. Cotton batt. Knife edge finish with red feather stitching. Blue plaid flannel back. Circa 1910, Pennsylvania, 72" x 74", excellent condition. $400.00 – 500.00.

A. Detail of center
B. Detail of corner
C. Detail of back

A

B

Trip Around the World hap.
Wool, corduroy, and velvet. Hand pieced, hand embroidered, hand tied. Embroidery on all seams. Cotton batt. Back brought to front edge finish. Salmon plaid flannel back. Circa 1920, Pennsylvania, 66" x 70", excellent condition. $450.00 – 600.00.
A. Detail of center
B. Detail of center
C. Detail
D. Detail of back

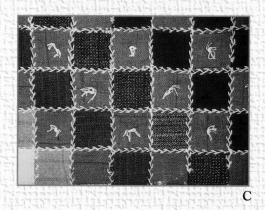

C

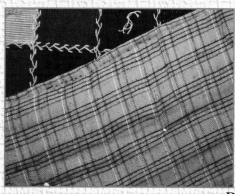

D

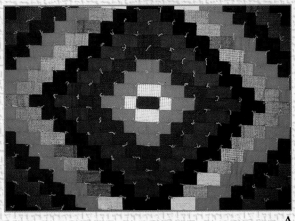

A

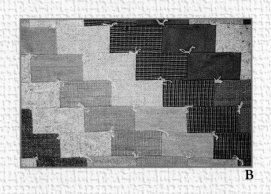

B

C

Trip Around the World hap.
Wool. Hand pieced, hand
tied. Cotton batt. Knife edge
with feather stitching. Pink
and blue plaid flannel back.
Note that was attached to
hap stated "For Lee W. Herber, Made February 1939 from
Mother Herber." Pennsylvania, 78" x 78", excellent condition. $500.00 – 600.00.

A. Detail of center
B. Detail of corner
C. Detail of back

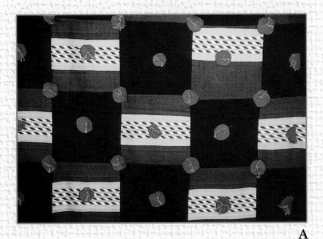

A

B

Squares with a Triangle border. Wool. Machine pieced, hand tied through red wool circles on both sides. Cotton batt. Red wool applied straight grain binding. Large floral decorative fabric back. Date embroidered on lower corner, 1941, Pennsylvania, 72" x 74", excellent condition. $500.00 – 700.00.
A. Detail
B. Detail of corner
C. Detail of back

C

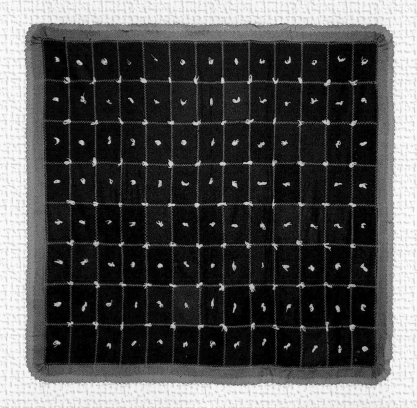

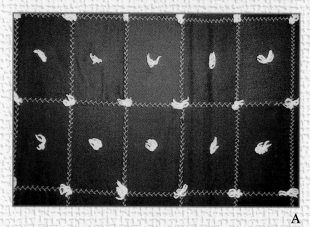

A

B

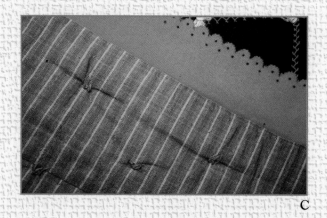

C

Rectangular One Patch hap. Wool. Machine pieced, hand embroidered, hand tied. Cotton batt. Blue and red wool decorative edge inserted between front and back. Plaid flannel back. Circa 1920, Pennsylvania, 64" x 64", excellent condition. $275.00 – 325.00.

A. Detail of blocks
B. Detail of corner
C. Detail of back

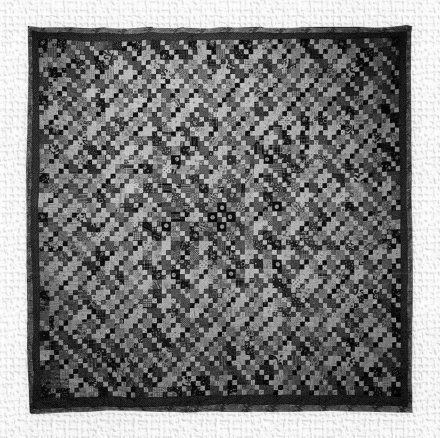

A

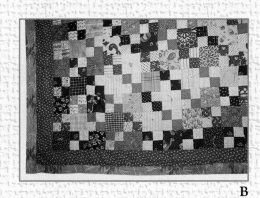

B

Four Patch and Squares.
Cotton. Hand and machine
pieced, hand tied. Cotton
batt. Back brought to front
edge finish. Printed fabric
backing. Circa 1890, Pennsylvania, 82" x 82", fair condition, some fabrics are brittle.
$350.00 – 400.00.
A. Detail of blocks
B. Detail of corner
C. Detail of back

C

Comforts

A

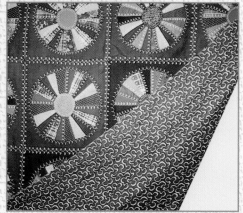

B

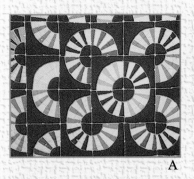

A

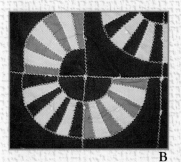

B

Top: Mennonite Dresden Plate with embroidery. Wool and cotton. Hand pieced, hand embroidered, hand tied. No batt. Knife edge and blanket stitched edge finish. Blue and cream wool and silk discharge print back. Circa 1900, 70" x 84", fair/good condition, some deterioration to stitching on edge and back. $600.00 – 800.00.

    A. Detail of blocks
    B. Detail and back

Bottom: Fans in a medallion set. Wool. Hand pieced, hand embroidered, hand tied. Embroidery on seams. Cotton batt. Knife edge finish. Green cotton back. Rare set. Circa 1900, Pennsylvania, 72" x 75", very good condition. $600.00 – 800.00.

    A. Detail of medallion
    B. Detail of corner

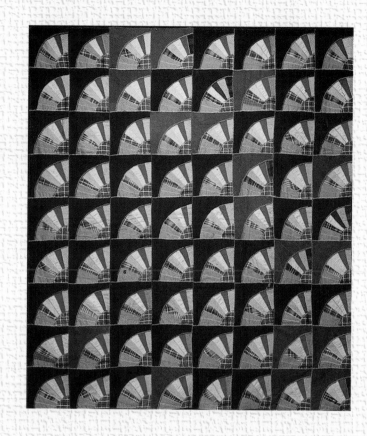

A

B

Top: Fans. Wool. Machine appliquéd, machine pieced, hand embroidered. Embroidery on seams. Cotton batt. Knife edge with blanket stitch. Pink cotton sateen back. Circa 1910, Pennsylvania, 68" x 80", excellent condition. $400.00 – 600.00.
A. Detail of fans
B. Detail of back

Bottom: Amish Fans. Wool. Machine pieced, hand embroidered, hand tied. Embroidery on seams. Thick blanket fill. Flannel applied binding. Green striped flannel back. Circa 1900, Pennsylvania, 68" x 80", good condition. $400.00 – 500.00.

Comforts

A

A

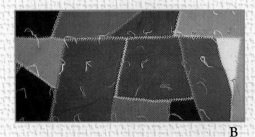

B

C

Top: String-pieced star. Cotton. Hand and machine pieced, hand tied. Wool batt. Red applied binding. Red paisley print back. Circa 1910, Pennsylvania, excellent condition. $350.00 – 450.00.

A. Detail

Bottom: Amish crazy patch. Wools and wool crepe. Machine pieced, hand embroidered, hand tied. No batt. Knife edge. Blue and red striped flannel back. Circa 1920, Pennsylvania, 62½" x 82", excellent condition. $600.00 – 800.00.

A. Detail
B. Detail
C. Detail of back

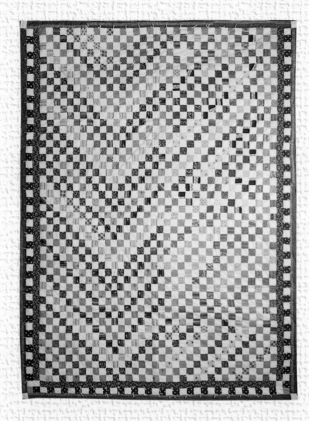

A

B

C

Top: Squares in One Patch design. Cotton. Hand and machine pieced, hand tied. Cotton batt. Knife edge finish. Pink and blue plaid back. Circa 1870s, top tied circa 1915, upstate New York, 62" x 84", excellent condition. $350.00 – 500.00.
A. Detail of corner
B. Detail
C. Detail of back

Bottom: LeMoyne Star. Wool. Machine pieced, hand tied. Cotton batt. Knife edge finish. Floral printed cotton back. Circa 1920, Arkansas, 68" x 82", excellent condition. $950.00 – 1,200.00.

Comforts

A

B

A

B

Top: Crib crazy patch Eight-pointed Star hap. Wool and cotton flannel. Machine pieced, hand tied. Cotton batt. Knife edge whip stitched. Plaid flannel back. Circa 1910, Pennsylvania, 39½" x 56", good condition. $250.00 – 350.00.

A. Detail
B. Detail of back

Bottom: Four Patch on point, reversible. Wool, silk, cotton, cotton sateen, rayon. Machine pieced, hand embroidered, hand tied. Wool blanket fill. Applied black bias wool binding. Sunshine and Shadow pieced blocks on back. Embroidered seams on both sides. Circa 1910, Pennsylvania, 71" x 71", excellent condition. $600.00 – 800.00.

A. Reverse
B. Detail of reverse

A

Top: One-piece Star hap.
Wool. Machine pieced, hand embroidered, hand tied. Cotton batt. Knife edge finish. Embroidered on all seams. Blue striped flannel back. Circa 1900, Pennsylvania, 69" x 81", excellent condition. $350.00 – 450.00.
A. Detail of block

Bottom: Eight-pointed Star with Octagon pieced center hap. Wool, cotton, silk, acetate blends. Machine pieced, hand embroidered, hand tied. Cotton batt. Knife edge finish. Blue flannel striped back. Circa 1920, 70" x 73", excellent condition. $400.00 – 500.00.

A

Top: Churn Dash hap. Wool. Machine pieced, hand tied. Cotton batt. Pieced applied binding. Brown striped flannel back. Circa 1930, Pennsylvania, 74" x 77", fair/good condition. $300.00 – 400.00.

A. Detail of corner

Bottom: Reversible string-pieced Kite shapes in Kaleidoscope arrangement. Cotton. Machine pieced, hand tied. Cotton batt. Striped applied straight grain binding. String-pieced Spiderweb on back. Circa 1930, Midwest, 66" x 66", excellent condition. $300.00 – 400.00.

A

Top: Reversible string-pieced Rocky Road to Kansas. Cotton. Machine pieced, hand tied. Cotton batt. Blue and white check applied straight grain binding. String-pieced Rocky Road to Kansas on back. Circa 1930, Midwest, 50" x 50", excellent condition. $350.00 – 450.00.
A. Detail of back

Bottom: Nine Patch hap. Upholstery weight velvets. Machine pieced, hand tied. No batt. Front to back edge finish. Red and beige striped cotton blanket back. Circa 1925, Pennsylvania, 67" x 74", excellent condition. $250.00.

Comforts

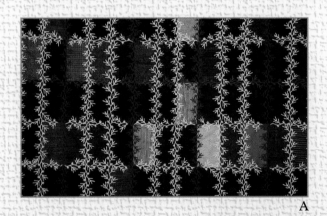

A

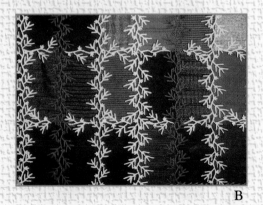

B

Pink, green, and yellow hap.
Wool. Machine pieced, hand
embroidered, hand tied. Cotton batt. Machine stitched
knife edge finish. Pale orange
and gray flannel plaid back.
Circa 1940, Pennsylvania,
65" x 67", excellent condition, very visual. $400.00 –
600.00.

A. Detail
B. Detail

Woven Bedcovers

Woven coverlets are one of the earliest forms of bedcoverings in the New World. Wool production existed prior to cotton. Dyes were readily available (blue especially). Indigo was one of our first cash crops. Looms were part of every day life. Coverlet weavers were professionals that traveled from client to client. Room and board was provided and often weavers used clients' materials. Frequently, professional weavers would indicate on one or more corner blocks, their names, the date woven, and sometimes the client's name. Wool and cotton often were combined in a coverlet. Linen and wool rarely were woven together.

While collecting coverlets has not been as active as quilts for instance, there has been growing interest. It has taken a long time for their prices to rise. They are steadily rising with more interest. Perhaps because they are wool, heavy, and subject to moths creating storage problems contributes to their limited collectibility. Many have suffered because they were used, and therefore, very few are in excellent condition. But, some still do exist.

Recent publications and scholarship have provided an opportunity for people to learn and become interested. They are available anywhere antiques are sold. Auctions often present opportunities for purchasing coverlets. Be aware of those that have been cut down; know where the fringes are supposed to be. Those having interesting color combinations or complexity of color, motifs, eagles, buildings, statements, etc. are always eagerly pursued by collectors.

Regional characteristics are more recognizable in coverlets than in other bed coverings. It is easier to determine the maker as there were relatively few professional weavers (mostly men) and they often signed their work or used a special motif or design attributed specifically to them. Sometimes records are available to indicate a specific area where a weaver traveled thus, enabling you to determine their identity.

This is not always possible because designs and styles were exchanged. The technique provides a limited range of possibilities and often designs were similar or the same or shared. Unless there is a particular unique design or design combination recognizable from one weaver then you cannot be sure without a signature. Most often a date, a county, a signature, and for whom it was made appears. Usually, if it is a name and a date, it will most often be the owner who commissioned the coverlet and not the maker.

The time span is short by comparison to other crafts. Their size, while not fitting today's beds, has prevented them from becoming a popular decorative item. However, their size lends itself to use as a throw on a sofa or daybed so many have suffered this fate. Some have fallen into the "proverbial throw pillow" which I choose to think of as the last efforts in preserving what was left of damaged coverlets. As in quilts, the greatest sins are created when individuals or decorators cut up textiles either not knowing or not caring about historical significance.

Care is a constant consideration when buying coverlets because they are wool. Displaying is not a problem if they are shown flat or on slant boards. Hanging is not a good idea unless the weight is relieved by supporting on a piece of muslin or other material stitched to the back with a rod pocket at the top. The coverlet should not be hung for long periods of time without resting — three months recommended at a time.

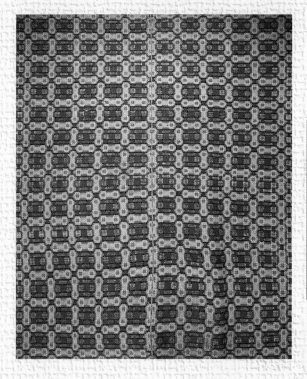

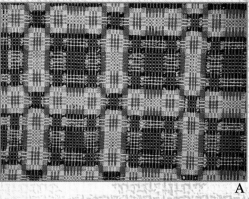

Black, red and tan cotton and wool overshot coverlet. One seam. Circa 1800, New England, 71" x 87", fair/good condition. $500.00 – 700.00.

A

A. Detail

A

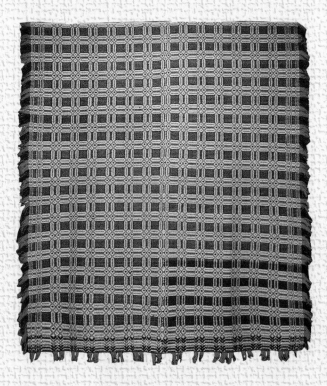

A

Top: Red, blue, and natural cotton and wool double weave coverlet. Geometric repeated pattern with pine tree border. Fringe on bottom only. One seam. Circa 1820, New England, 73" x 82", very good condition. $600.00 – 800.00.

    A. Detail of corner

Bottom: Red and green cotton and wool overshot coverlet. Fringe on three sides. Top is bound in a printed cotton. Fox Chase variation. One seam. Circa 1830, Pennsylvania, 72" x 82", excellent condition. $800.00 – 1,000.00.

    A. Detail of corner

A

B

C

Top: Red and blue wool jacquard coverlet. Exotic birds with their young in a nest. Urns of flowers and a Christian and heathen double border. One seam. Fringe on three sides. Top is hemmed. Circa 1850, 79" x 90", excellent condition. $1,200.00 – 1,500.00.
A. Detail of birds
B. Detail of urns
C. Reverse side detail of border

Bottom: Teal, blue, green, and red wool and cotton overshot coverlet. Fringe on three sides. Top is hemmed. Geometric pattern. One seam. Circa 1840, Pennsylvania, 76" x 86", excellent condition. $750.00 – 900.00.

A

A

Top (one quarter view): **Indigo, red, burgundy, and natural double weave wool and cotton coverlet.** One seam. Medallions with leaf and floral border. Fringe on bottom only. Hemmed top. Circa 1850, 74" x 88", excellent condition. $1,200.00 – 1,500.00.

    A. Detail of border

Bottom: Blue and white wool jacquard coverlet. Signed "E. Guile, Bethany Genesee, NY, 1838." Roses with birds and stars. No fringe. Hemmed at top and bottom. One seam. 86" x 86", excellent condition. $1,500.00 – 1,800.00.

    A. Detail of signature block

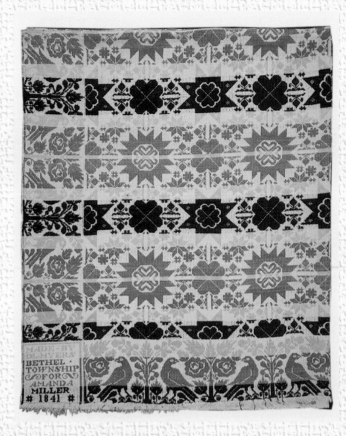

A

Top: Blue, red, yellow, and natural wool and cotton double weave coverlet. Stars and flowers with birds and roses in border. Signature block, "Made by D. Myers, Bethel Township For Amanda Miller 1841." Fringe on three sides. Wool tape binding on top. One seam. 71" x 93", excellent condition. $900.00 – 1,200.00.
A. Detail of signature block

Bottom: Blue and white jacquard wool and cotton woven coverlet. Center medallion, eagles with a ribbon, animals, and birds. Floral border with small temple-like building. No fringe. No seam. Circa 1860, 77" x 85", good condition. $600.00 – 800.00.
A. Detail

A

A

B

C

D

Rust, navy, and natural wool and cotton double weave coverlet. Four Roses pattern. Fringe on three sides. One seam. Corner block dated 1847, Pennsylvania, 84" x 100", excellent condition. $900.00 – 1,200.00.

A. Detail of border
B. Detail of corner block on dark side
C. Detail of light side
D. Detail of corner block on light side

A

Top: Blue and white wool and cotton jacquard woven coverlet. Leaves and sunbursts. Border has urns and flowers and corner block on right and left. Fringe on bottom only. Hemmed top. One seam. Dated 1855, 72" x 92", excellent condition. $1,200.00 – 1,500.00.
A. Detail of corner block

Bottom: Blue and red wool and cotton beiderwand woven coverlet. Center medallion with turkeys in each corner. Fringe on three sides. No seam. Circa 1855, Pennsylvania, 87" x 90", excellent condition. $750.00 – 900.00.
A. Detail of center
B. Detail of turkeys in corners

A

B

Clothing

Children's

Collectors have always been drawn to diminutive forms. The most obvious reason is space constraints, but the less obvious is the charm associated with miniatures. Whether it is furniture or other objects, scaled down examples have always been sought after by collectors.

Children's clothing, for a variety of reasons, holds this appeal. In the past, children were dressed like adults. Much of their clothing is scaled down versions of full-sized adult attire. Perhaps the appeal is much the same as collecting objects from the past but here the attempt to recall childhood memories has a particular significance.

Very few of these items survived by comparison to what was produced. By their very nature, having been made for children, would explain their limited lifespan. Hard use as well as being handed down from one generation to the other contributed to their demise. Those that have survived are usually those made for special occasions rather than every day. These, as well as other objects associated with children, appeal to collectors today. Often these objects are used in interior decorating schemes as decorative accessories.

As a result, their popularity continues to drive the market up and their availability down. It is still possible to obtain items. But when anything becomes fashionable, newly made items replicating the old, even made of period fabrics often find their way into the market place. Here is where you need to be aware of what you are doing. Educate yourself or buy from a reputable dealer who will stand by their merchandise. Auctions are a good source, but dealers who buy directly from households are your best source. Cultivate a relationship with a reputable dealer and you should have many opportunities not only to buy but also to learn.

B

A

Child's dress. Cotton floral printed on decorative weave. Circa 1840, New Jersey. $175.00.

A. Detail
B. Detail

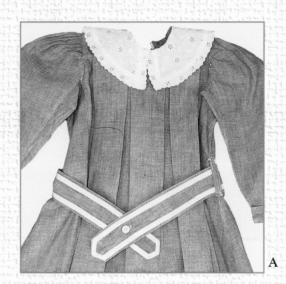

A

Top: Child's blue chambray dress with fancy lace collar for either boy or girl, and a pair of cotton dress socks. Circa 1900, New England. $150.00.
A. Detail

Bottom: Two pairs of Amish children's knee socks. Woven wool with decorative motifs at the top. Circa 1920, Pennsylvania. $45.00 and $95.00.
A. Detail

A

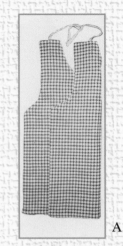

A

Top: Child's beige and brown woven cotton check bib. Circa 1900, New England. $25.00.

A. Detail

Bottom: Boy's navy blue woolen coat with white decorative cording design. Circa 1900, New England. $150.00.

A. Detail

A

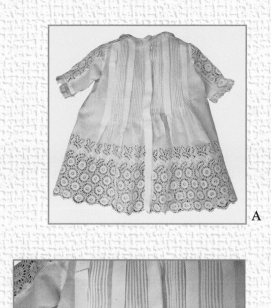

A

B

C

Top: Fancy infant dress. White cotton. Circa 1890, New England. $150.00.
A. Back
B. Detail of back
C. Detail of lace along bottom of dress

Bottom: Two pairs of Amish mittens. Knitted wool. Small pair in stripe. Large pair in a geometric pattern. Circa 1920, Pennsylvania. $25.00 and $45.00.

Quilted Petticoats

Often petticoats are offered for sale because they can exhibit decorative quilting. As items of apparel, they were often two to three layers joined by a running stitch. This garment was functional in that it provided warmth but it also provided another surface to be adorned with designs just like a quilt. It is important to remember that the quilting provided stability for the batting. While keeping the batting stationery, it also created design opportunities.

Although these garments were worn underneath outer clothing, they were often very elaborate. Wool, cotton, and silk are represented in the examples shown. Some are extremely utilitarian with the simplest parallel lines of machine quilting; others are more elaborate. Both types are pictured. Collectors value examples of unique, interesting fabrics, styles, decorative quilting patterns, and condition. Also high on the list would be those that reflect the era in which they were made and the quality of the quilting, no matter whether it is hand or machine. In summation, beautiful color, beautiful fabric, beautiful quilting, very good workmanship, good condition, and rarity are the factors you should consider when selecting petticoats for your collection.

A

B

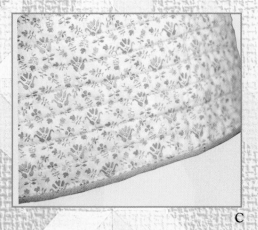

C

D

Brown printed cotton reversible petticoat. Machine quilted in horizontal lines. Hand-applied woven tape binding along bottom. Circa 1880, New England, 27" waistband, 37½" length, 42" bottom width, very good condition. $225.00 – 275.00.

A. Detail
B. Reverse side
C. Detail of hem
D. Detail of waistband

A

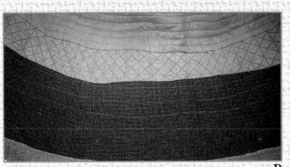

B

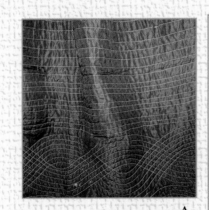

A

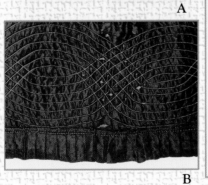

B

C

Top: Beige polished cotton petticoat. Machine quilted in horizontal bands and a 10½" grid divided diagonally along the bottom. Applied crocheted decorative edge 1¾" along the hem. Lined with a 7½" coarse woven homespun cotton plaid. Circa 1880, New England, 21" waistband, 33" length, 37½" bottom width. Very good condition. $250.00 – 300.00.
A. Detail of hem
B. Detail of lining

Bottom: Black silk petticoat with yellow machine quilting. Quilted in horizontal lines, double cable. Applied ruffle edge at bottom with a black velvet lining the ruffle. The petticoat lining is a black printed cotton. Circa 1890, Pennsylvania, 19" waistband, 34" in length, 33" bottom width, very good condition. $250.00 – 300.00.
A. Detail
B. Detail of cable and hem
C. Detail of printed and velvet lining

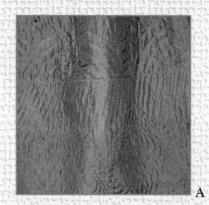

A

C

B

D

Burgundy silk reversible petticoat. Signature on interior of waistband, "Reifsnyder," written in ink. Hand-quilted fans, feather wreaths, parallel lines filling the cable area. Double crosshatch in center of feather wreaths. Knots are obvious on the surface. Circa 1860, Pennsylvania, 30" waistband, 28" in length, 40" bottom width, very good condition. $300.00 – 350.00.

A. Detail of quilting
B. Beige interior with tape signature
C. Detail of hem
D. Detail of signature tape

A

B

Black cotton sateen petticoat. Parallel line hand quilting with wide horizontal band at top and cable along the bottom. Crocheted wool band at hem. Two color black printed lining. Circa 1910, Pennsylvania, 26" waistband, 38" in length, 42" bottom width, very good condition. $225.00 – 275.00.

A. Detail of waistband
B. Detail of hemline
C. Two black printed fabrics of lining

C

A

B

Top: Black wool petticoat with red quilting. Parallel lines, zigzag, floral motif. Applied red crocheted band at bottom. Black silk and black printed fabric lining. Circa 1890, Pennsylvania, 24" waistband, 33" in length, 38" bottom width, very good condition. $225.00 – 275.00.
    A. Detail of quilting
    B. Detail of lining

Bottom: Wool red and black plaid child's petticoat. No quilting and no lining. Circa 1910, Pennsylvania, 12" waistband, 26" in length, 39" bottom width, very good condition. $75.00 – 125.00.

Aprons

One might think that aprons are an odd thing to collect. However, when you look at their purpose and place in everyday life, you begin to see their importance, functionally and fashionably. They create a fascination and that in itself, leads to curiosity. Curiosity is where collecting starts.

Aprons can be as interesting as any other area of pursuit once you start viewing them as artifacts of our cultural past. Realizing that they were used to protect clothing from soil, does not seem such a big deal today, but remembering the arduous chore of doing laundry before machines, brings about a different attitude toward these useful items of clothing. Many activities required men, women, and children to wear protection for their clothing. This protection took the form of aprons made of appropriate material for the intended purpose. In some cases, aprons were elevated and became fashionable and in style rather than just utilitarian.

Many major historical museum collections feature fashion, and aprons are an important aspect of our cloth heritage. While it may not be possible to obtain aprons from our distant past, it is still possible to acquire aprons representing the nineteenth and early twentieth centuries. Many auctions include kitchen cloth items and usually among them will be an apron or two.

A familiarity with fabric production as well as styles from different periods is helpful when collecting items of clothing. Of particular interest about early aprons is their design. Before purchased patterns were available, individuals designed their own aprons according to their own needs. In many cases, the stature of the individual maker is easily identified by the shape and size of the apron.

Although most aprons were made of cotton, the variety in style and print makes each one attractive and somewhat distinctive — a treat for collectors.

Skirt style child's apron. Printed cotton with porcelain button fastener. Circa 1840, New York, 27" long. $150.00 – 200.00.

A. Detail

A

A

A

Top: Skirt style adult apron. Brown and blue check. Woven cotton. Circa 1880, New England. $125.00.

A. Detail

Bottom: Skirt style adult apron. Orange, blue, and white checked woven cotton. Circa 1880, Pennsylvania. $100.00.

A. Detail

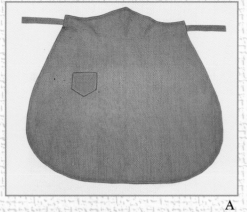

A

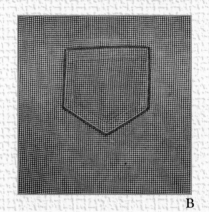

B

A

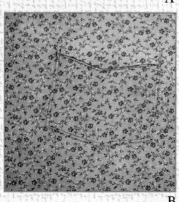

B

Top: Skirt style adult apron. Black and white checked cotton. Circa 1910, Pennsylvania. $75.00.
A. Detail
B. Detail

Bottom: Jumper style adult apron. Black and white mourning print. Cotton. Circa 1900, Pennsylvania. $125.00.
A. Detail
B. Detail

A

A

Top: Jumper style adult apron. Black and white check. Woven cotton. Circa 1890, Pennsylvania. $125.00.
A. Detail

Bottom: Jumper style adult apron. Blue and white check. Woven cotton. Circa 1890, Pennsylvania. $125.00.
A. Detail

A

A

Top: Jumper style adult apron. Woven blue and white plaid. Cotton. Circa 1880, New England. $100.00.
A. Detail

Bottom: Short skirt style adult apron. Blue and white woven check with white embroidery at the hem. Cotton. Circa 1910, New England. $95.00.
A. Detail of embroidery

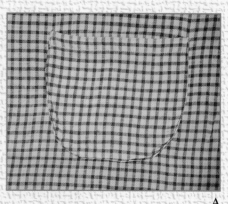

A

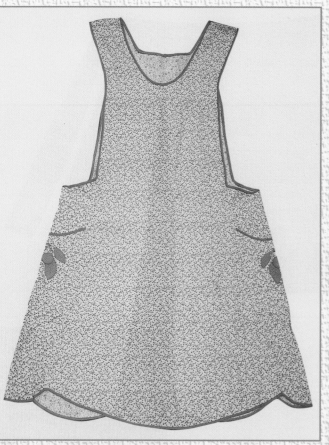

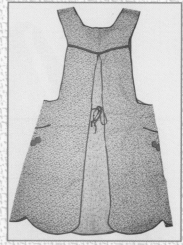

A

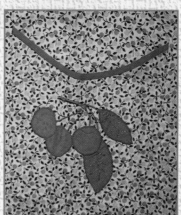

B

Top: Short skirt style adult apron. Blue and white woven check with pink rickrack edge. Cotton. Circa 1910, New England. $75.00.

A. Detail

Bottom: Smock style adult apron. Red, green, gold, and white cotton print. Red rickrack trim and appliquéd cherries on the pocket. Circa 1930, Midwest. $125.00.

A. Detail
B. Detail

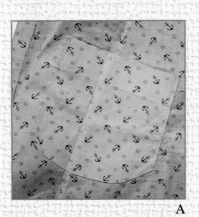

A

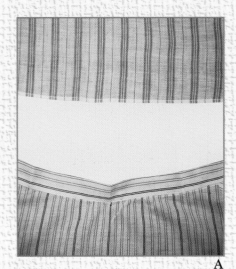

A

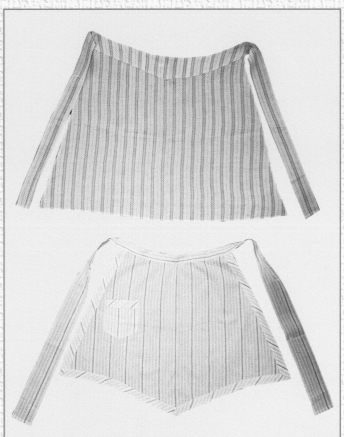

Top: Short skirt style adult apron. Red and white shirting anchor print. Cotton. Circa 1920, Midwest. $75.00.
A. Detail

Bottom: Two short company aprons. Both are blue and white striped cotton shirting material. Circa 1920, New England. $75.00 each.
A. Detail

A

A

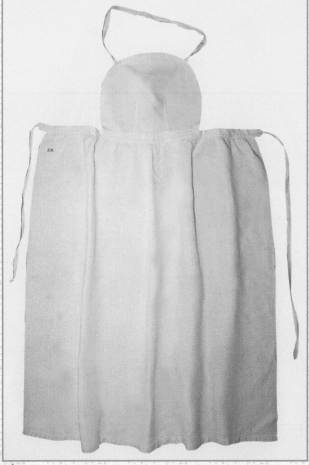

A

Top: Short skirt style adult apron. Checkerboard pattern patchwork cotton. Circa 1930, Midwest. $85.00.

A. Detail

Center: Skirt style adult apron. Linen and cotton Swedish apron with fine embroidery and lace. Circa 1890. $250.00.

A. Detail

Bottom: Shaker skirt style apron with bib. White linen. Embroidered in red cross stitch, "A.M." Circa 1900, Cantebury, New Hampshire. $250.00.

A. Detail

Bonnets

It is understandable why some collectors have become interested in bonnets purely because of their aesthetics. As many of the photos show in this section, bonnets are very beautiful objects; even the very simple utilitarian examples. Displayed on elevated forms, they become elegant shapes and make remarkable decorative accents. Bonnets have a wide range of styles and appeal from very fancy, expensive, and fashionable types to the very simple and functional. Even with the latter, the attention to style is evident.

Their intended function was simply to protect from the elements — most often the sun. Bonnets are present in one way or another in all cultures. They developed out of necessity, but always with attention to style. It is obvious that even the simplest form gave the maker an opportunity to create an object of necessity while paying attention to style that would enhance the wearer. The idea of framing the face — surrounding the features with soft fabrics and often adornment — presents an ideal situation for fashion statement, while still solving a practical problem.

We will present here, those examples made of similar materials and representing the same periods as other items in this book. The same criterion for dating and evaluating is true of bonnets; identifying cloth from different periods and recognizing styles, as in other areas of costume. Before the mass production of clothing, these examples represent the maker's own design choices.

Geographical location can be an important identifying factor as well as group or religious sect. Some of these bonnets are Amish and Mennonite and exhibit particular cloth and construction styles associated with these specific peoples. They are, therefore, recognizable because of their particular appearance and frequently, their regional characteristics. The behavioral restrictions imposed for religious beliefs are reflected in the style of clothing within these groups. While the functional aspect remained the same, a simpler, less ornamental style developed, with recognizable characteristics. Simple shapes, stylized by a restricted use of decoration, so as not to appear vain, but elegant even within these limitations.

Bonnets are not readily available as usual antique shop inventory. Dealers that regularly offer costumes, fabric, linens, etc. would be the most common source. People involved in reenactment (historic) activities are usually the most interested customers. The same criterion for purchasing bonnets or any other antique is condition, condition, condition!

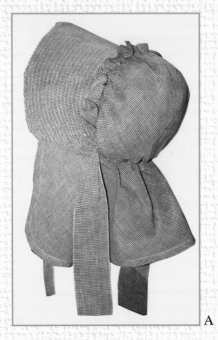

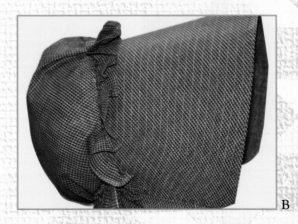

Blue gingham adult work bonnet with machine quilted visor and ruffle to protect the neck against the sun. Last quarter nineteenth century, Pennsylvania. $125.00.

A. Detail back view
B. Close-up of visor showing the quilting pattern

A

B

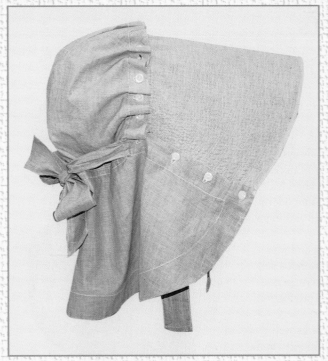

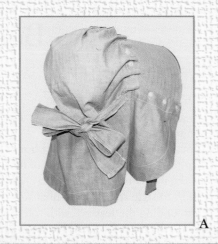

A

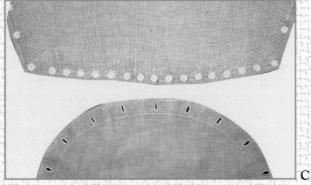

C

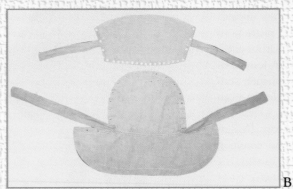

B

A

Top: Green chambray adult work bonnet. Button construction enables bonnet to be disassembled for laundering. Extension to protect the neck against the sun. Last quarter nineteenth century, Pennsylvania. $125.00 – 150.00.

A. Back view
B. Each bonnet piece arranged flat
C. Detail of buttons and buttonholes

Bottom: Black silk adult dress bonnet. Mennonite. Circa 1890, Pennsylvania. $150.00.

A. Close-up of quilting on the visor

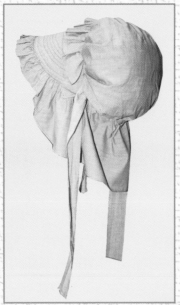

A

B

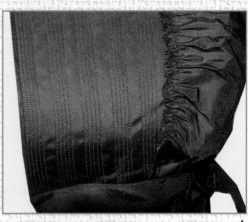

A

Top: Pink chambray adult work bonnet. Extension to protect the neck against the sun. Last quarter nineteenth century, Pennsylvania. $125.00 – 150.00.
A. Back view
B. Close-up of machine quilting on the visor

Bottom: Black silk adult dress bonnet. Mennonite. Last quarter nineteenth century, Pennsylvania. $150.00.
A. Detail of the quilting on the visor

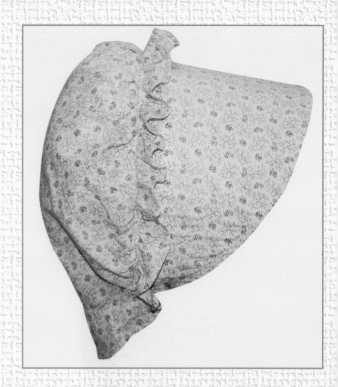

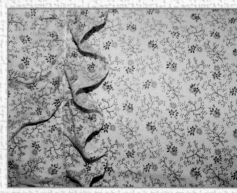

A

A

A

Top left: Sheer silk adult black summer bonnet. Mennonite. Last quarter nineteenth century, Pennsylvania. $150.00.

A. Detail of the quilting on the visor

Top right: Child's yellow calico bonnet. Cotton. Last quarter nineteenth century, Pennsylvania. $95.00 – 110.00.

A. Detail of the ruffle and construction

Bottom: Black Amish adult wool bonnet. Last quarter nineteenth century, Pennsylvania. $150.00.

A. Three-quarter view showing the detail of construction and quilting on the visor

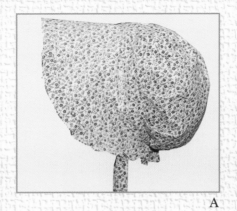

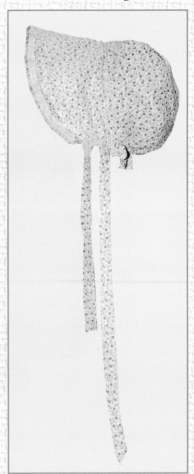

A

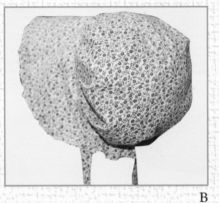

B

A

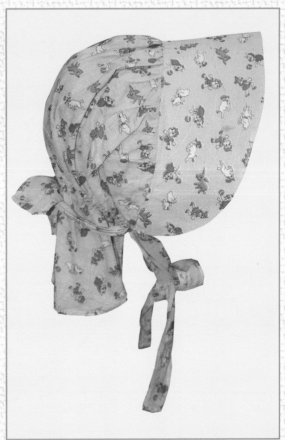

Top: Yellow calico child's bonnet. Cotton. Last quarter nineteenth century, Pennsylvania. $95.00 – 110.00.
A. Side view
B. Back view

Bottom: Youth yellow novelty print bonnet. Cotton. First quarter twentieth century, Pennsylvania. $110.00 – 125.00.
A. Detail showing the novelty print

A

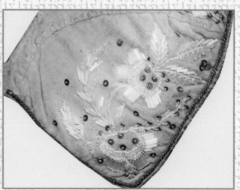

A

Top: Shaker child's bonnet in brown dyed straw. Brown velvet interior and trim. Circa 1900, Canterbury, New Hampshire. $350.00 – 500.00.
A. Back view

Infant Bonnets
Left: Velvet. Beaded and decorated with tiny steel cut sequins. Embroidered with metallic thread on edge. Late eighteenth century – early nineteenth century, European. $150.00 – 200.00.
A. Detail

Right: Cotton. Beaded in blue floral design with steel cut sequins. Late eighteenth century – early nineteenth century, European. $150.00 – 200.00.

Linens

Bed

Bed linens have experienced a similar fate as that of table linens. They represent a past era when great attention to detail was common practice. Luxurious and fashionable homes require time, talent, taste, and the means to afford such standards. The Industrial Revolution in the nineteenth century provided the opportunity by creating the largest and wealthiest middle class in history. This wealth provided the means to support lifestyles that demanded and afforded the production of elegant furnishings as well as the opportunity to use them. The talents and techniques available to produce these items were on a much smaller scale. Prior to this time, these luxuries were only afforded by the very rich or nobility. Even though the machine age created time-saving devices that produced finished products from raw materials, these items still required a great deal of handwork. The demands created jobs for many people and the results were not only the items themselves, but the passing down of skills and techniques necessary to create the details on these fine linens that otherwise might have been lost.

History often repeats itself, but never exactly the same way. Since the Industrial Revolution, we have only evidenced one similar period — the "computer age." Many fortunes were made and as a result, luxurious life styles evolved. This time the demand was not met nor satisfied by willing and knowledgeable craftsmen so the demand has to be satisfied with whatever antique pieces can be acquired.

The bedroom however, still is a very personal and private place. It provides an opportunity to express great love, affection, care, and luxurious comfort for loved ones. In the past, tremendous pressure was placed on women to produce fine linens prior to marriage, even before they were betrothed. Here we see a great flowing of complex designs, monograms, and pride of workmanship with little regard to the time spent on creating these items. So, engaged by the romantic notions of love, marriage, home, and family, these items are produced without thought of time spent or compensation. Today that same expression of love may still be the motivation; however, contemporary life styles, while providing the means to purchase these items, could not possibly provide the time or the dedication to create comparable objects.

It is amazing how many of these linens were produced and have survived. Their survival poses an interesting question: Why? The most obvious would be perhaps many women did not marry or that much of what was produced was never put into household use either by the maker or preceding generations. Perhaps their care became too great or they became unfashionable. For whatever reason, they survive and many are available today.

Linens varied according to bed sizes until bed sizes were standardized in the early twentieth century. This limits current use for some items but because antique beds were large, many of these furnishings can be used today. The interest in antique linens has also created a need for modern manufacturers to produce new items that are available and complement the old.

The interest in antique bed linens continues as decorating magazines consistently publish articles and photos showing their uses. Even in today's busy life styles, people will take the time to create luxurious beds using elaborate linens. Even if a busy life does not allow for personal use, a guestroom will often be furnished luxuriously to provide a special person the experience of luxury and the romance associated with the past. Bed linens will often be found in shops specializing in table linens. Again, condition is of the utmost importance. Cloth has a limited life span. Proper care is important in prolonging its life for current as well as future generations to enjoy.

A

Bride's sheet. Linen and cotton. Lace along top and 24" down each side to turn back over covers. Circa 1880, New England, 93" x 105", excellent condition. $200.00 – 250.00.

A. Detail

A

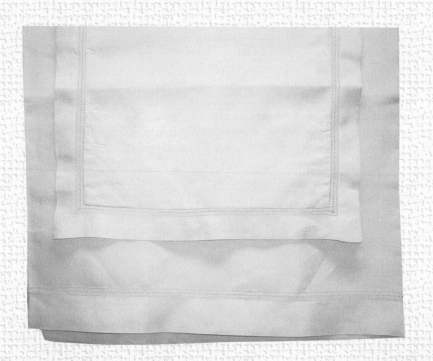

A

Top: Sheet. Linen. Matching pair of pillow covers, 24" x 37½". Circa 1880, New England, 90" x 92", excellent condition. $200.00 – 250.00 set.

A. Detail

Bottom: Sheet and matching pair of pillow shams. Linen. Circa 1890, New England, sheet 89" x 108", shams 24" x 36", excellent condition. $225.00 – 275.00.

A. Detail

A

B

C

Top: Sheet. Cotton. Elaborately decorated top with church, angels, floral, and vine designs. Circa 1880, New England, 86½" x 102", excellent condition. $200.00 – 250.00.
A. Detail
B. Detail
C. Detail

Bottom: Sheet. Linen. Circa 1880, New England, 94" x 101", excellent condition. $150.00 – 175.00.

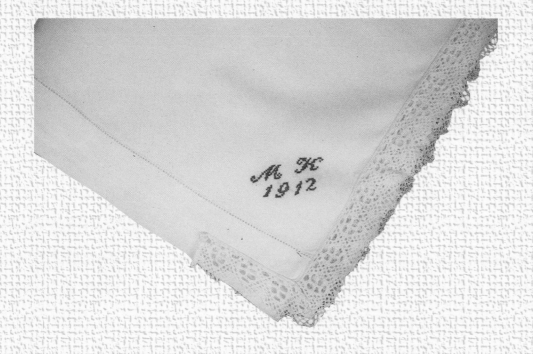

A

B

Top: Single sheet. Cotton. Monogrammed M.H. and dated 1912. Lace across top and 6" down each side. New England, 58" x 78", excellent condition. $85.00 – 100.00.

Bottom: Pair of pillow shams. Cotton. Circa 1890, New England, 32" square, excellent condition. $125.00 – 150.00 pair.

A. Detail
B. Detail

A

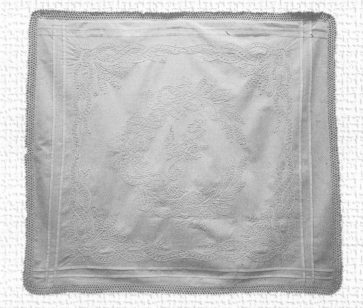

B

Top: Pair of pillow toppers.
Linen. These were strictly decorative and were placed on top of the pillows. Circa 1890, Pennsylvania, 32" x 36", excellent condition. $250.00 – 300.00 pair.
A. Detail
B. Detail

Bottom: Pair of pillow toppers.
Linen. These were strictly decorative and were placed on top of the pillows. Circa 1890, 29" x 31", excellent condition. $250.00 – 275.00 pair.
A. Detail

A

A

B

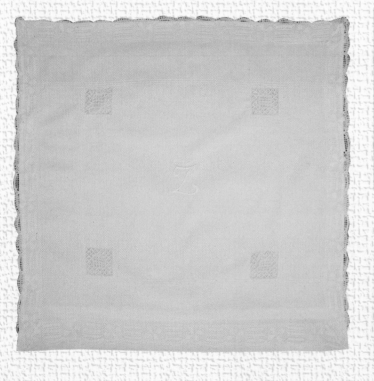

A

B

Top: Pair of pillow shams.
Linen. Circa 1880, England,
24" x 34", excellent condition. $225.00 – 275.00 pair.
A. Detail
B. Detail

Bottom: Pair of pillow shams. Cotton. Circa 1890,
New England, 32" square,
excellent condition. $225.00
– 275.00 pair.
A. Detail
B. Detail

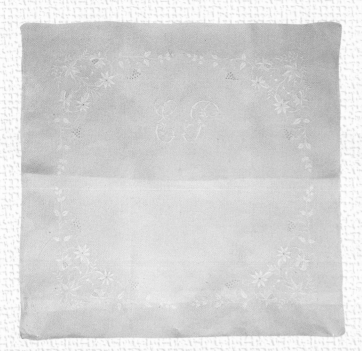

A

A

Top: Pair of pillow shams. Linen. Circa 1880, England, 26" x 27", excellent condition. $250.00 – 300.00 pair.
A. Detail

Bottom: Pair of pillow toppers. Cotton. Red work embroidery, "I Slept and Dreamed That Life Is Beauty, I Woke and Found That Life Was Duty." Circa 1890, New England, 27" x 24", excellent condition. $125.00 – 150.00.
A. Detail

Pillow cases. Cotton. Various edge treatments. Circa 1890 – 1900, 21" x 30", excellent condition. More elaborate: $50.00 – 75.00 pair. Less elaborate: $35.00 – 50.00 pair.

Pillow cases. Cotton. Various edge treatments. Circa 1890 – 1910, 21" x 30", excellent condition. Less elaborate to more elaborate: $25.00 – 45.00 pair.

A. Detail
B. Detail
C. Detail

A

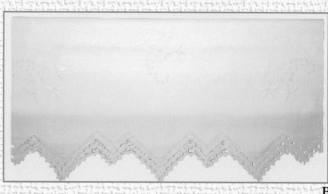

B

C

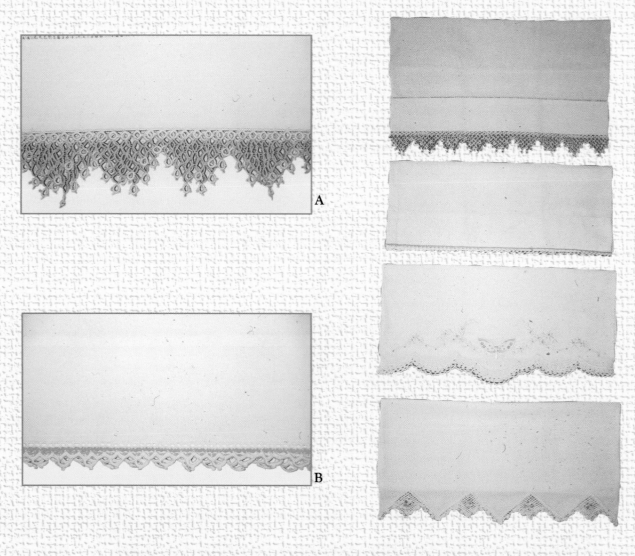

Pillow cases. Cotton. Various edge treatments. Circa 1900 – 1920, 21" x 30", excellent condition. Less elaborate to more elaborate: $25.00 – 35.00 pair.
A. Detail
B. Detail
C. Detail
D. Detail

Linens – Bed

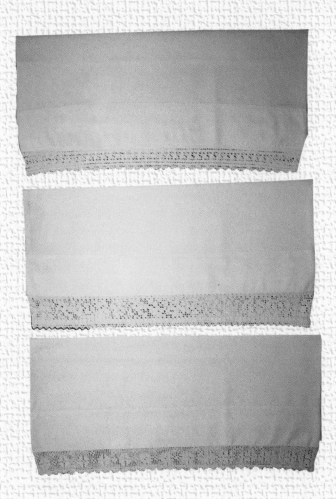

A

Top: Pillow cases. Cotton. These represent those standard size bought cases with hand-decorated edges — usually crocheted. Circa 1920 – 1940, 21" x 30", excellent condition. $20.00 – 30.00 pair.
A. Detail

Bottom: Pillow cases. Cotton. Novelty pillowcases preprinted, crocheted, embroidered. Price depends upon designs and complexity of pattern as well as quality of workmanship. Circa 1930 – 1940, 21" x 30", excellent condition. $30.00 – 50.00 pair.
A. Detail

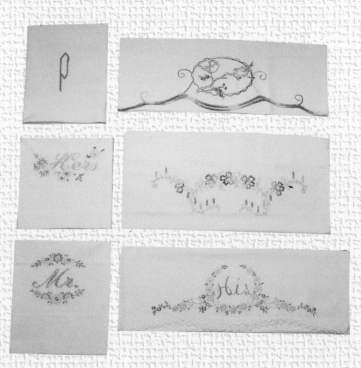

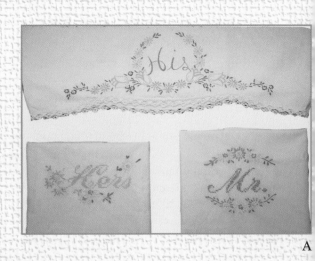

A

Table

This group of items has always been of interest to collectors. There are shops all over the world that specialize in this type of cloth. Antique linens have always represented household furnishings of great interest and demand. They reflect a time when attention to detail and decoration was of the utmost importance and the time and labor to produce them unfathomable by today's standards.

Setting a table symbolizes status, taste, and love of family. People often went beyond their means to set an elegant table, if not for everyday, then for company or special occasions. Cloth has always symbolized luxury and nowhere do we see it more than in table linens of the past. Especially in the late nineteenth century, the Victorian era saw a great deal of wealth distributed among an enormous cross section of the population. The Industrial Revolution created the largest and wealthiest middle class and upper middle class ever seen at any time in history.

The Victorians created not only tableware for specific purposes, but also a great emphasis was placed on elaborate table and household linens. The economy provided the wealth necessary to produce those items being demanded by this newfound prosperity. The handwork evidenced in these products revitalized an industry, luckily still retaining the skills to produce such objects.

Although the market for these goods varies with current trends, there has always been enough demand for skilled craftsmen to keep these techniques alive. Much of what is produced today is not made domestically.

Collecting antique table linens for use in the home is just one aspect of collecting. Some collect different examples of each technique just to have them represented in their collection. Their value when compared to the cost of replacing items today with comparable materials and skill makes them very reasonable.

Most of what is available today is representative of the mid- to late nineteenth century. Life styles after World War I reflect a simpler life. Women's lives were altered by wartime and they did not necessarily return to spending full time in the home. Only the very wealthy continued to employ laundresses who cared for fine linens. Simpler ways of life, less time spent on fussy linens allowed for streamlining a new lifestyle.

They were not discarded; however, but saved and handed down from one generation to another and are still in evidence in most household inventories today. Perhaps each generation intends to use them, but then the reality of washing and ironing usually retires them once again, to the buffet for another generation.

In the last 30 years there has been a growing interest in food preparation and presentation. Perhaps the computer age like the Industrial Revolution produced such affluence for so many that we are seeing history repeating itself. Gourmet cooking, James Beard, Julia Child, Martha Stewart, had a tremendous influence on changing America's interest in food and entertaining. A generation was inspired and encouraged and as a result, entertaining at home, cooking, and setting a beautiful table became popular again. This resulted in a renewed interest in antique table lines. No matter where you go in the world, you will find shops specializing in these items. While it is not as easy today as it was years ago, there are still opportunities to collect. Prices have increased over the years because supply is limited and demand is high but the interest continues. When looking at fine linens you cannot help but be impressed by the skill, craftsmanship, time, and patience it took to create them.

They are usually available through auction houses specializing in estate auctions. There are shops that specialize in fine linens where if you make it known what you are looking for, they will call you when they acquire such an item. Often shops selling these items are the best source because people will often go directly to them to sell such items. These are the best sources of new merchandise and visiting these shops often is advisable.

Again, condition, condition, condition is the most important factor. Gaining the knowledge to buy wisely can often be acquired by cultivating a regular customer relationship with a reputable dealer. Looking at a wide variety of items and selecting items to suit your taste that are also selected from experience, is a more knowledgeable position. It is also necessary to learn to care for these items. A good dealer is often the best source of this information also. Caring for these objects is one of the pleasures of owning and collecting.

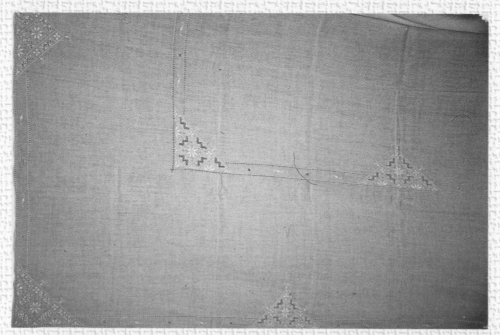

Top: Table cloth. Linen
Circa 1880, New England
68" x 104", excellent condition. $250.00 – 300.00.
      A. Detai
      B. Detai

Bottom: Table cloth. Linen
Circa 1890, New England
66" x 82", excellent condition. $300.00 – 350.00.
      A. Detail of corner

A

B

A

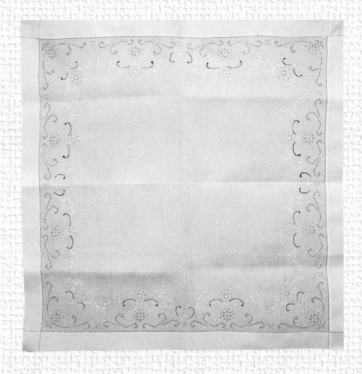

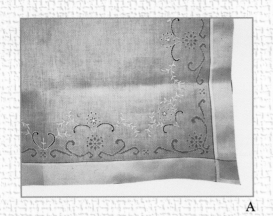

A

A

Top: Table cloth. Linen. Circa 1890, New England, 34½" x 35½", excellent condition. $100.00 – 125.00.
A. Detail of corner

Bottom: Table cloth. Linen. Circa 1890, New England, 41½" x 41½", excellent condition. $125.00 – 150.00.
A. Detail

A

B

A

C

B

Top: Round table cloth.
Linen. Circa 1880, 51" diameter, excellent condition.
$150.00 – 200.00.
A. Detail
B. Detail

Bottom: Center table cloth, linen set. 12 placemats and 12 napkins. Circa 1910, New England, excellent condition.
$250.00 – 300.00.
A. Detail
B. Detail
C. Detail

144

A

B

Table Runner. Linen. Circa
1910, New England, 50" x
17", excellent condition.
$110.00.
A. Detail
B. Detail

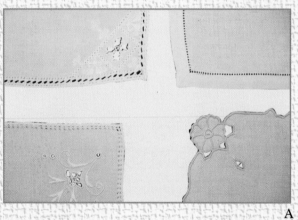

A

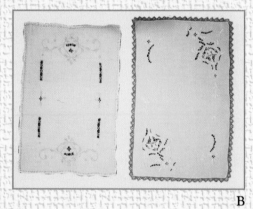

B

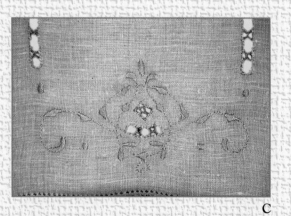

C

D

Sets of eight placemats.
Linen. Value varies according
to age, complexity of design
and condition. Circa 1890 –
1930, New England, approximately 12" x 17", excellent
condition. $18.00 – 25.00
each placemat.
A. Detail
B. Detail
C. Detail
D. Detail

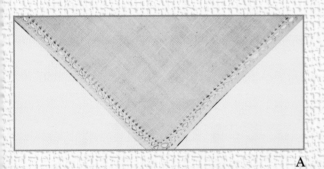

A

B

Napkins. Linen. Most often sold in sets of 8 – 12. Value depends upon size, condition, workmanship and complexity of design. Circa 1900, New England, approximately 16" square. $8.00 – 15.00 each napkin.
A. Detail
B. Detail
C. Detail

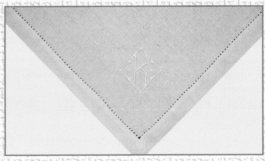

C

147

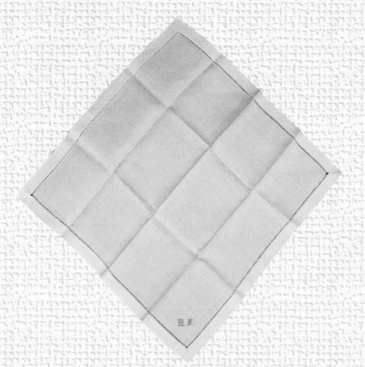

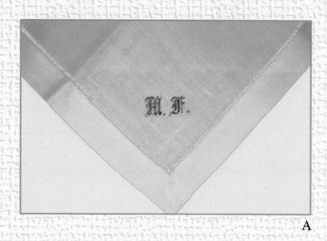

A

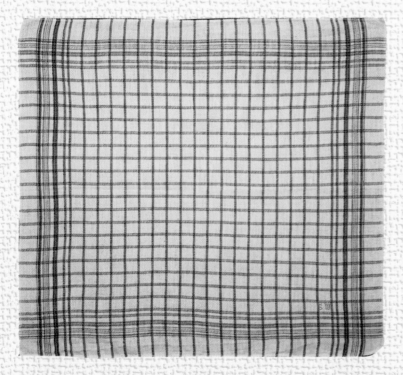

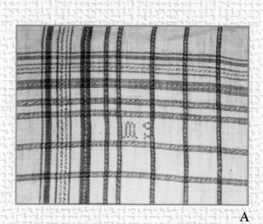

A

Top: Napkins. Linen. Inked monograms. Circa 1900, New England, 14" square, excellent condition. Set of six, $75.00 per set.
A. Detail

Bottom: Napkins. Cotton and linen. Hand woven, finished and stitched in red with the initials "S.W." Circa 1870, New England, 19¾" x 17½", excellent condition. Set of eight. $125.00.
A. Detail

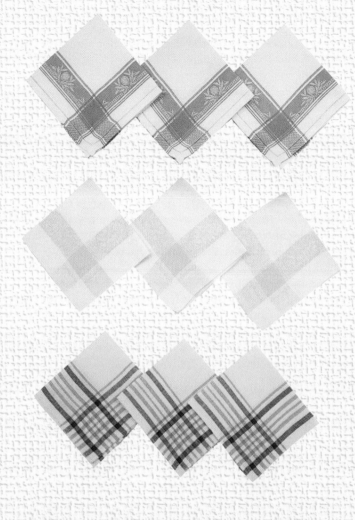

Top: Napkins. Cotton. Circa 1920, New England, 14" x 14", excellent condition. Set of six. $40.00 – 50.00 per set.

Bottom: Turkey red and white table cloth. Cotton. Circa 1890, New England, 60" square, excellent condition. $250.00 – 275.00.

Fabric

Originally, woven cloth was for protection from the elements and for warmth and security. Eventually cloth became decorative when the warp was combined with a different color weft, and a geometric design or pattern resulted. This probably was the beginning of the industry we recognize today.

Techniques for applying design on the surface of woven cloth soon followed. This allowed freedom from woven geometric patterns to unlimited design possibilities. Simple stamping or block printing was the first method of transferring color to the surface of cloth. At this point the simple aspect of maintaining the design on the cloth becomes necessary. Experimentation with pigments and mordant was necessary to achieve permanence of design. With improved technology came more sophisticated combinations of color and pattern and technique.

From the infancy stage of cloth production, it represented status and luxury. For some, its purpose was strictly utilitarian, but for others with wealth and station, it also served to increase enjoyment and as personal decoration.

Through history, fabrics have always reflected fashion styles and trends of the time in which they were produced. The evolution of design, the immense variety of color and pattern, the recognition of an industry that presents beautiful works of art, and the documentation of our history in this unique form is why textile historians, museums, costume collectors, and historical societies are interested in gathering these cloth artifacts.

Cloth has a relatively short lifespan compared to other objects. As a result, there is only a small representation from the past. This scarcity automatically creates a healthy market, i.e. demand. However, collecting antique fabric is less expensive than purchasing quilts and other large textiles. It is more practical to store and yet satisfies the need for those who respond to the tactile sensuality of cloth.

Some people are drawn to collecting antique fabric just because of the sheer beauty of cloth; others are interested in those fabrics because of historical or political significance, or perhaps novelty prints, special techniques such as woven designs, finishes, or prints, style (art deco, floral, toile, etc.), a particular time period, or whatever satisfies your personal need.

It is important to note that America, England, and France all copied prints from one another. Fabrics were reproduced, almost from the beginning of the mechanized printing industry. Often, the changes that were made to the reproduction fabrics were so subtle that it is extremely difficult to tell which is the original older piece and which is the reproduction. In some cases, there were no changes — printing companies would reprint the same patterns exactly as they had been decades earlier. These practices can cause confusion and difficulty when determining the date of textiles.

Toile

Toile is recognized by the scenic copperplate printed patterns dating from the 1770s.

French mulberry prints. Set of four scenes. Circa 1780 – 1810, purchased in France. $375.00 – 475.00 set.

A

B

C

Details of French mulberry prints.
A. Detail of scene
B. Detail of scene
C. Detail of scene
D. Detail of scene

D

Toile 1795 – 1825.
English or French. Values are per repeat and vary depending on size of repeat, color, complexity, and popularity of design.

Bottom:
$150.00 – 200.00.
A. Detail

A

Fabric – Toile

B

C

A

Top: $250.00 – 325.00.
A. Detail
B. Detail
C. Detail

Bottom: $225.00 –
275.00.

A

A

Top: $250.00 – 300.00.
A. Detail

Bottom: $250.00 – 300.00.
A. Detail

Chintz

Chintz fabrics shown range from circa 1825 to 1845. Values vary depending on color, size of repeat, subject, and condition. Originally a painted cloth from India, chintz became popular in Europe as decorative furnishing fabric used for beds and windows. It was rapidly reproduced in France and England.

Values per repeat, unless otherwise noted.

A

B

Chintz:
Circa 1825 – 1845 unless otherwise noted.

Fragment of English pillar print. Woven tape along one edge in matching colors.
Circa 1825 – 1835. $250.00.
A. Detail
B. Detail of woven tape

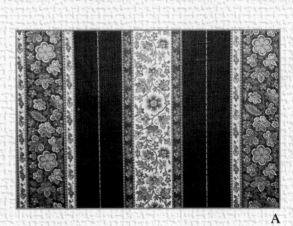

A

Top: $250.00 – 300.00 per yard.

Middle: $250.00 – 300.00 per yard.
A. Detail

Bottom: $100.00 – 125.00.

A.

Top left: $100.00 – 125.00.

Top right: $100.00 – 125.00.
A. Detail

Bottom: $100.00 – 125.00.

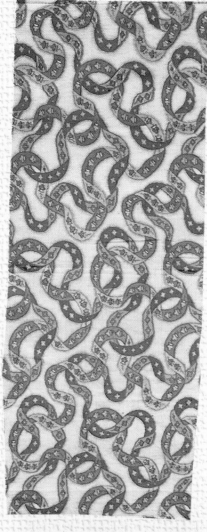

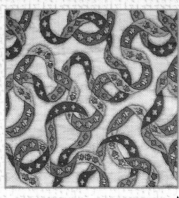

A

Top left:
$250.00 – 300.00 per yard.

A. Detail

Top right: $100.00 – 125.00.
each.

Bottom:
$250.00 – 300.00 per yard.

Fabric – Chintz

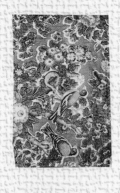

Top left:
$100.00 – 125.00.

Middle:
$125.00 – 150.00.

Bottom:
$75.00 poor condition.

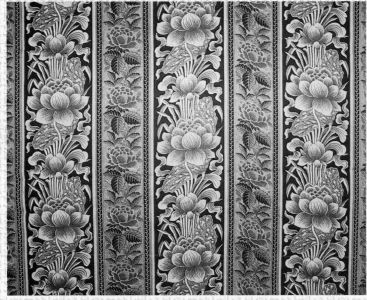

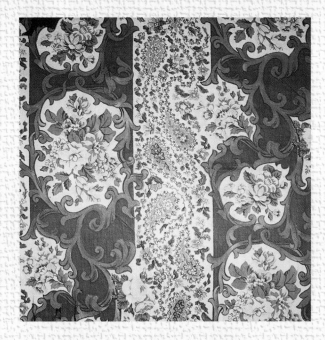

Top left:
$250.00 – 300.00 per yard.

Top right:
$250.00 – 300.00 per yard.

Bottom left:
$250.00 – 300.00 per yard.

Bottom right:
$100.00 – 125.00.

Top left:
$75.00.

Top right:
$250.00 – 300.00 per yard.

Middle:
$100.00 – 125.00.

Bottom left:
$75.00 fragment.

Top:
$100.00 – 125.00 each.
A. Detail of floral stripe

Bottom:
$250.00 – 300.00 yard.
A. Detail of floral stripe
B. Detail
C. Detail of bird

A

A

C

B

Fabric – Chintz

Top left:
$250.00 – 300.00 per yard.

Top right:
Twentieth century reproduction
of fabric in lower left photograph.
$200.00 per yard.

Bottom left:
$75.00 fragment.

Bottom right:
$250.00 – 300.00 per yard.

Top left:
$175.00 – 200.00 per yard.

Chintz
Circa 1890 – 1920.
Top right:
$150.00 – 175.00 per yard.

Bottom:
Twentieth century reproduction
of top left photograph.
$150.00 per yard.
A. Detail

Printed Cotton

Fabrics in this section are all cotton and are valued per one-half yard.

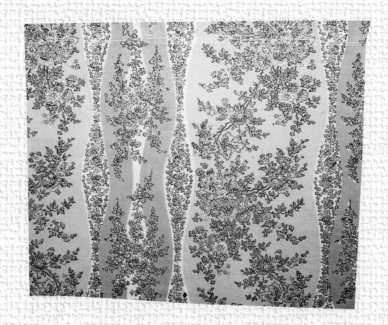

Pre-1840
Top left: $150.00.

Top right: $150.00.

Bottom: $150.00.

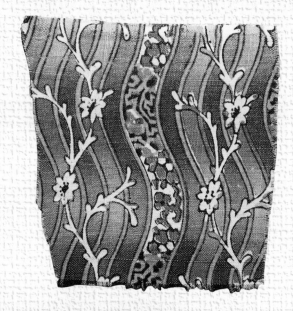

Top left: $150.00.

Top right: $25.00.

1830 – 1860
Middle: $100.00 – 125.00.

Bottom: $100.00 – 125.00.

Fabric – Printed Cotton

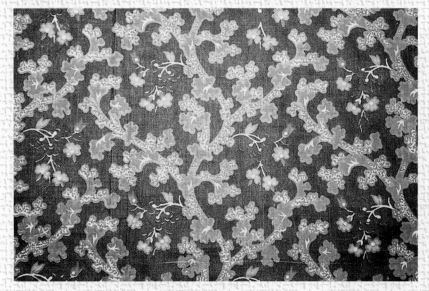

Top left: $100.00 – 125.00.

Top right: $75.00 – 100.00.

Middle: $75.00 – 100.00.

Bottom: $75.00 – 100.00.

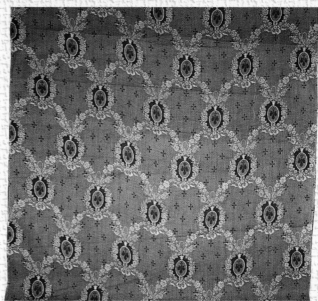

A

1880 – 1900
Top: $125.00.

Middle: $50.00 – 75.00.

Bottom: $175.00.
A. Detail

Fabric – Printed Cotton

A

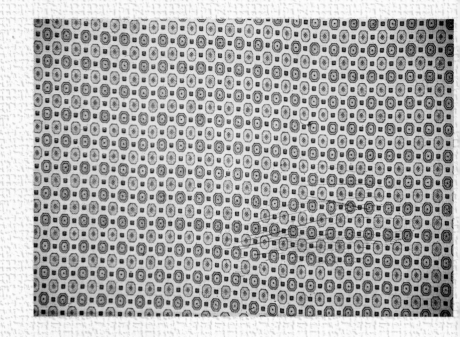

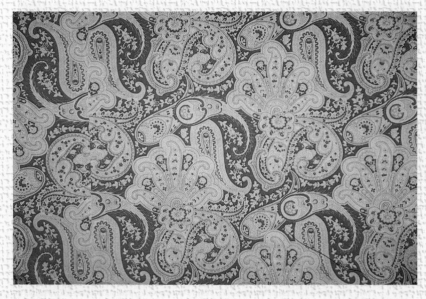

Top: $50.00.
A. Detail

1900 – 1920
Middle: $50.00.

Bottom: $50.00.

Similar Colors or Print Styles

Values are by one-half yard cost unless otherwise noted.

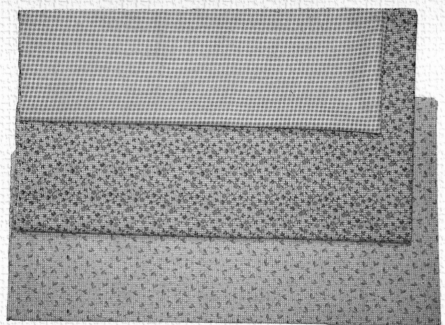

Circa 1870, double pinks.
Top: $50.00 – 75.00.

Bottom: $50.00 – 75.00.

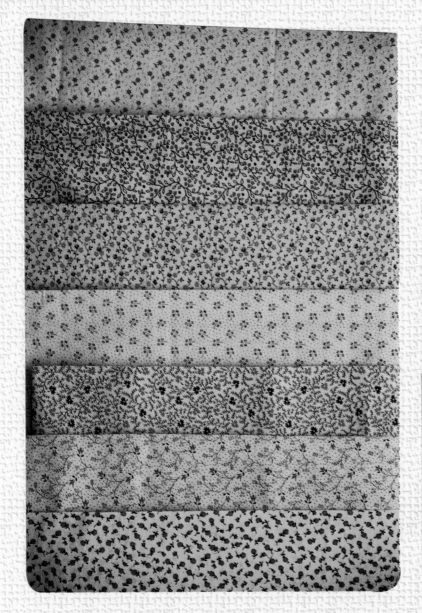

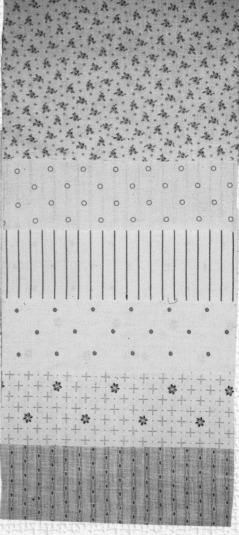

Circa 1870, yellow prints.
Top: $50.00 – 75.00.

Circa 1880 – 1910, shirting.
Bottom: $50.00 – 75.00.

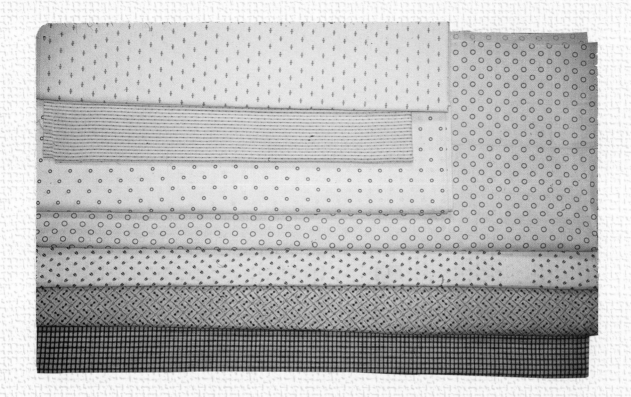

Top: $50.00 – 75.00.

Circa 1880, mourning
prints and plaid.
Bottom: $50.00 – 75.00.

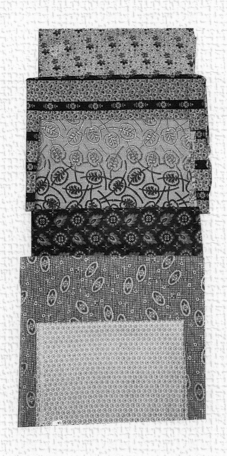

Top: $50.00 – 75.00.

Circa 1860 – 1880,
brown prints.
Bottom: $75.00.

Top: $75.00.

Bottom: $75.00.

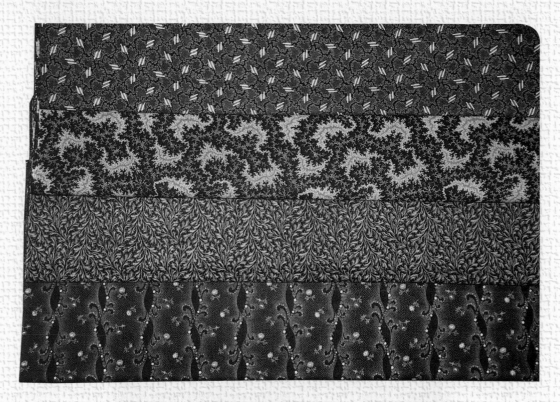

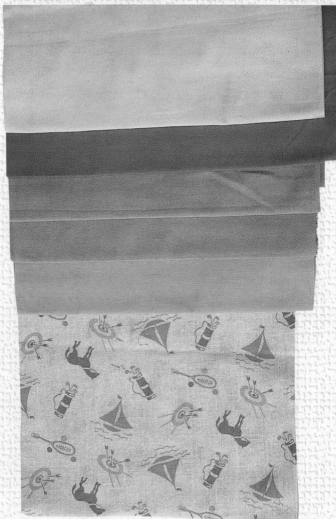

Circa 1890, pink, maroon,
and black prints.
Top: $50.00 – 75.00.

1924 – 1950, feed sacks.
Bottom: $18.00 – 25.00,
general range of solids
and various prints.

Saleman's Samples

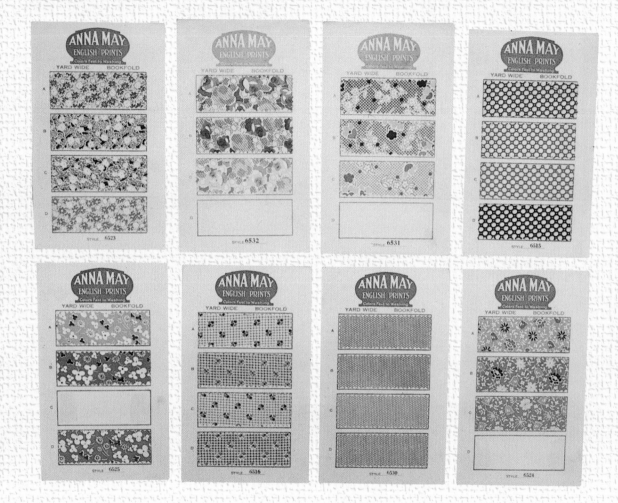

Salesman's Sample Cards. "Anna May English Prints" advertised as "Yard Wide" and "Bookfold." Circa 1935, excellent condition. $15.00 each.

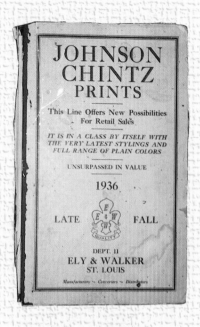

A

B

Salesman's sample book, Johnson Chintz Prints. Ely & Walker, St. Louis, 1936, 8" x 13" x 1¼", excellent condition. $350.00 – 400.00.

A. Detail
B. Detail

Garibaldi or Robe Prints

"Giuseppe Garibaldi, 1807 – 1882, was an Italian war hero, who was elected to the Italian Parliament in 1874. He remained a popular hero of Italians the world over. His son, Ricciotti Garibaldi, 1847 – 1924, was an Italian patriot who fought with his father in Italy and for Greece against the Turks. Giuseppe's grandson, Giuseppe or Peppino Garibaldi, 1879 – 1950, was an Italian general who fought for Britain in the Boer War, commanded Greek troops in the Balkan Wars, and in the First World War commanded a legion of Italian volunteers. His opposition to Mussolini caused him to immigrate to the United States in 1924." — *The Columbia Encyclopedia*, Columbia University Press, page 795, ed. By William Bridgwater and Seymour Kurtz.

"Sears also referred to its red and black prints, small and large scale, as Garibaldi cloth, a probable reference to the Italian hero whose followers wore red shirts. Garibaldi prints, robe prints, or black on red prints are strong clues to the 1875 – 1925 era when both the large scale and small-scale versions were popular for quilt backing, sashing, for whole-cloth tied comforters, and for patches in scrap quilts." — *Clues in the Calico*, Barbara Brackman, EPM Publications, Inc., 1989.

It is easy to understand why prints associated with the Garibaldi family might have enjoyed popularity for many years. Values are per one-half yard.

Both fabrics, $50.00.

A

Top: $50.00.

Middle: $50.00.
A. Detail

Bottom: $35.00.

Political or Patriotic Prints

Values are by one-half yard unless otherwise noted.

Top: Fabric is from the **Crystal Palace Exhibition of 1851** featuring Queen Victoria and the Prince of Wales Plume. 29¾" x approximately 20" repeat, excellent condition. $175.00 – 224.00.
A. Detail

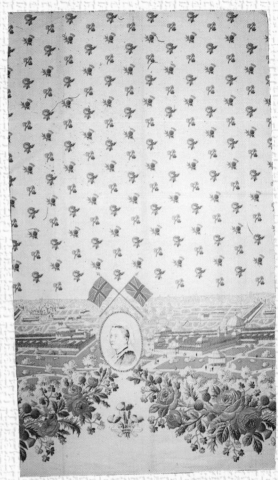

A

Bottom: Charles A. Lindbergh print commemorating the successful Lindbergh flight from New York to Paris in the Spirit of St. Louis, in 1927. Medium weight plain weave cotton. 1928 – 1933, about 36" wide, unused condition. $100.00 – 125.00.
A. Detail

A

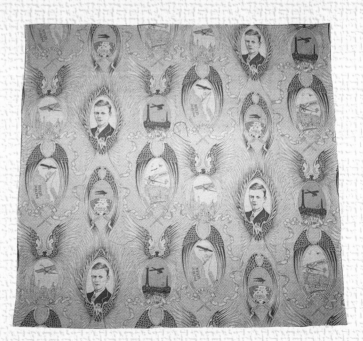

Fabric – Political or Patriotic Prints

A

Top left: Eisenhower toile. Screen printed in various dark ground colors such as red, blue, and brown, in the middle of the twentieth century. Designed by Elisabeth Draper and Katherine Sturges Knight and produced 1956 – 1960 in New York by F. Schumacher & Co. First Lady Mamie Eisenhower had a dress made from this fabric. $50.00 – 75.00.

A. Detail

Top right:
Centennial print. 1876. $75.00 – 100.00.

Bottom: Printed panel featuring James Gillespie Blaine (1830 – 1893) **and General John A. Logan** (1826 – 1886). In 1884, Blaine received the Republican nomination for President, with Logan as his Vice Presidential running mate. Logan, later, was the founder of Memorial Day. The Democrat, Grover Cleveland, was victorious in the election. Blaine later became Secretary of State under Benjamin Harrison. Printed on thin cotton. Circa 1884, excellent condition. $50.00 per repeat.

Rugs

Recycling cloth into articles of household use is as old as cloth itself. Since cloth is one of the most highly prized materials providing comfort in our lives, it is not surprising that its use continues until the end of its survival.

The production of floor coverings created techniques for converting remnants or used bits of cloth into useful objects for the floors. Floors have always provided an opportunity for useful as well as decorative touches in the home. Rugs served many purposes. They added warmth to a room, they absorbed sound, comforted the feet, and trapped dirt. Along with all the practical purposes, they also provided a canvas for personal aesthetic expression. Even a simple rag rug woven on a loom with leftover bits of clothing torn into strips provided an opportunity to create a variety of interesting striped designs. Different colors of warp added another dimension. Joining these lengths together provided a floor covering which added another design possibility.

Hooked rugs, constructed of strips of material pulled through a foundation, produced another style. This form of rug making is referred to as rug hooking and traditionally used wool yarn or fabric such as wool or cotton.

Braided rugs were also a style of floor covering born of necessity and often made of leftover materials from other projects. This technique also provided an opportunity to use old woolen materials found in used clothing. The good parts were cut into strips and braided. The braids were then laced together to form a flat surface that could be very attractive on a floor. Although using worn and recycled materials first made these home furnishings, the countless designs created by color, style interpretation, etc. can be very decorative in a home today.

Currently, it is fashionable rather than practical to produce these items for home decoration. Most designs are purchased or even printed on surfaces so a certain element of individual creative expression has been lost to commercial mass manufacturing and marketing.

It is for this reason that the original, one of a kind design of years ago are sought after by collectors. These objects are readily available in antique shops around the country. The unusual and rare find their way to the best dealers and usually that is where you will find the most interesting examples. Many of these rugs have been mounted to hang on walls. This appears to be a good practice because many fine old examples are not capable of withstanding current cleaning techniques necessary when rugs are used as floor covering. Vacuums, for instance, are too strong, shaking is not advisable, nor is washing. There are those that can withstand current use; you just have to be sensible and make decisions about those that can and cannot withstand daily use.

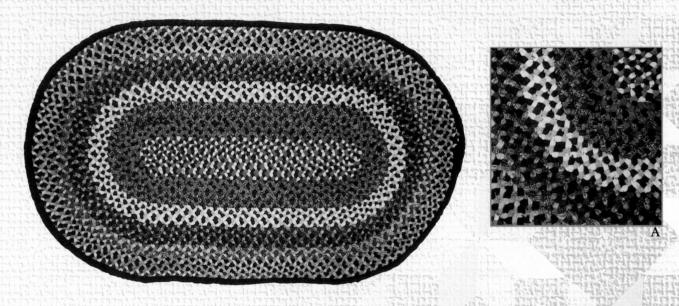

A

Braided rug. Hand laced. Wool. Circa 1900, New England, 27" x 47". $175.00.

A. Detail

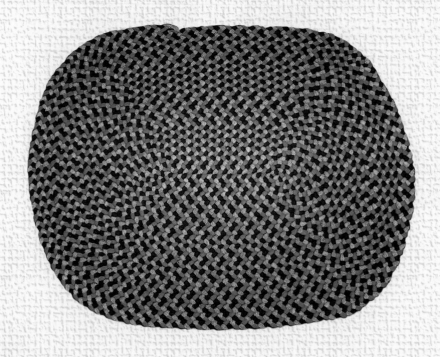

Top left: Braided rug. Wool. Circa 1920, New England, 34" x 50". $175.00.

Top right: Rag rug. Woven. Cotton. Circa 1880, Pennsylvania, 23" x 38". $35.00.

Left: Braided rug. Wool. Circa 1940, Mennonite, Pennsylvania, 31½" x 42". $150.00 – 175.00.

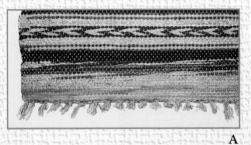

A

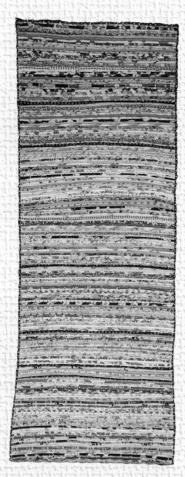

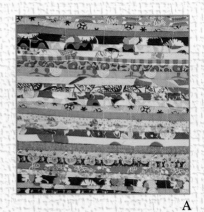

A

A

Top left: Rag runner. Woven. Cotton. Circa 1880, Pennsylvania, 24½" x 96". $250.00.
A. Detail of the end

Top right: Sewn foundation rug. Cotton strips. Circa 1935, California, 26" x 80". $350.00.
A. Detail

Bottom: Rag runner. Woven. Cotton. Circa 1940, Pennsylvania, 26" x 102". $300.00 – 350.00.
A. Detail

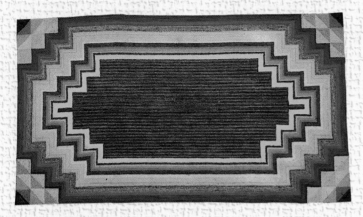

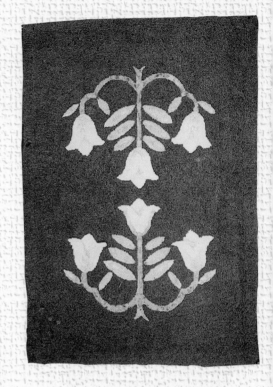

Top left: Hooked rug. Geometric pattern. Wool. Circa 1940, New England, 33" x 54". $600.00.

Top right: Hooked rug. Tulips pattern. Wool. Circa 1890, Pennsylvania, 18" x 25". $225.00.

Middle: Hooked rug. Wirehaired terrier puppy. Wool. Circa 1930, origin unknown, 20" x 35". $750.00 – 900.00.

Bottom: Hooked welcome rug. Wool. Circa 1920, New England, 24" x 36". $1,500.00 – 1,800.00.

Towels

Towels are both functional and decorative. At one time, only those representing fine handwork were valued. Now there is so much interest in decorating with country and primitive styles, even the homely common homespuns are popular. The quality is still there, even years after they were produced so they are practical, but most of the time they are just collected and displayed in open kitchen cupboards as decorative accents. The earlier, the better. Natural homespun linen with striped edges, the type that was woven in one long length and cut according to need, or those that were woven individually with stripes at either end seem to be the most popular today.

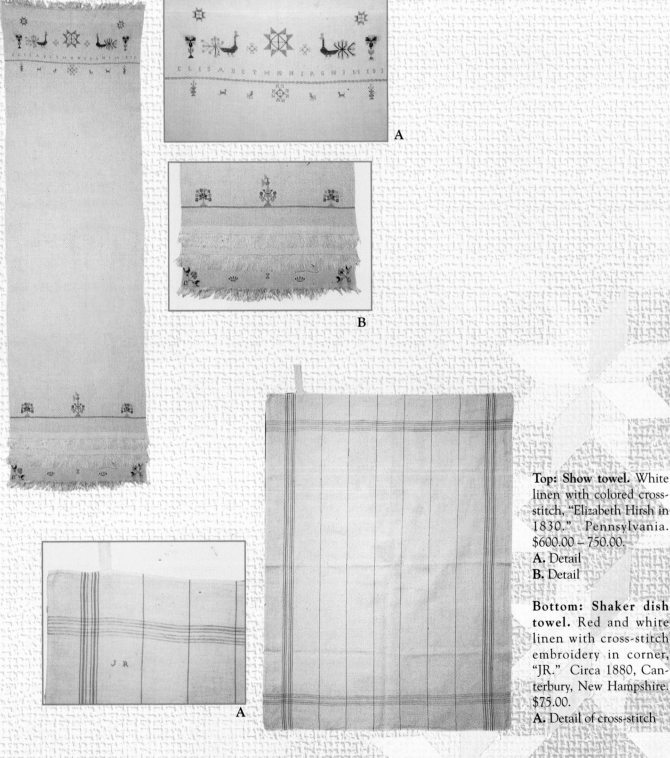

A

B

A

Top: Show towel. White linen with colored cross-stitch, "Elizabeth Hirsh in 1830." Pennsylvania. $600.00 – 750.00.
A. Detail
B. Detail

Bottom: Shaker dish towel. Red and white linen with cross-stitch embroidery in corner, "JR." Circa 1880, Canterbury, New Hampshire. $75.00.
A. Detail of cross-stitch

Towels

A

A

A

A

Top left: Homespun linen towel with blue decorative woven stripes on both ends. Circa 1860, New England. $45.00.
A. Detail

Top right: Homespun natural linen towel with blue and yellow decorative woven stripes on edges. Circa 1860, New England. $45.00.
A. Detail

Bottom: Striped towels. Reds, oranges, blues, greens, and yellows on white cotton. Circa 1930, New England. $25.00 each.
A. Detail

A

Top left: Homespun blue and white plaid cotton towel. Circa 1860, New England. $25.00.

Top right: White cotton fancy hand towel with drawn work edge decoration and monogram, "HM." Circa 1890, New England. $45.00.

Bottom: Group of three white cotton guest towels with red monograms and red and white decorative embroidery. Circa 1870, New England. $25.00 each.
A. Detail of red work

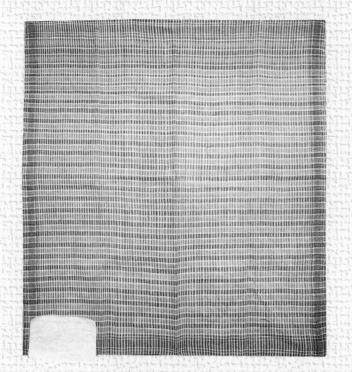

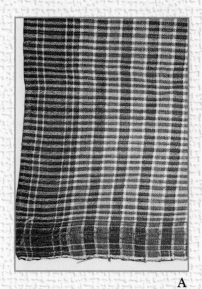

A

B

Linen homespun necker-chief. Blue and brown plaid. Made by Samuel Haile (born in Rhode Island in 1780 and moved to Washington County, New York, about 1805). Circa 1820. $150.00 – 200.00.

A. Detail
B. Detail

About the Authors

Bobbie Aug has been collecting antique quilts and other textiles for nearly forty years. Her appreciation of quilt history eventually grew to include a love of quiltmaking. Bobbie enjoys making quilts in both traditional and contemporary styles. Her experiences as an antique quilt dealer, quilt store co-owner, appraiser, and judge have helped her focus on creating a textile collection that brings her enjoyment and a sense of accomplishment. She especially likes to collect unique representatives of traditional styles. To contact Bobbie about judging, teaching, lecturing, or appraising information: Bobbie A. Aug, P.O. Box 9654, Colorado Springs, CO 80932. E-mail: qwltpro@msn.com or visit her website at www.BobbieAug.com.

Gerald Roy comes to quiltmaking from a fine arts background. After receiving an MFA in painting, he taught art for 10 years in Oakland, California. Growing up in Massachusetts, he developed a deep love and appreciation for American antiques. Eventually he and his late partner, Paul Pilgrim, opened a gallery on the west coast. Ever since his first serious quilt purchase in 1969, Gerald has been involved in an all-consuming quest to collect the finest examples of quilts that exemplify the unique esthetic nature of the maker. Now, relocated back on the east coast, the quest continues. To contact Gerald about judging, teaching, lecturing, or appraising information: Gerald Roy, P.O. Box 432, Warner, NH 03278. E-mail: Pilgrimroy@tds.net.

Both authors are nationally known quilt historians, lecturers, and teachers of workshops about quiltmaking and quilt history. They have been engaged in the textile business for well over 60 cumulative years and have previously sold antique textiles in their own retail stores. Bobbie and Gerald have authored and co-authored over ten books about quiltmaking, including *Vintage Quilts: Identifying, Collecting, Dating, Preserving & Valuing*, published by Collector's Books. In addition to being quiltmakers and certified quilt appraisers, they enjoy working on the board of directors for the American Quilter's Society Quilt Appraiser Certification Committee, testing and certifying appraisers of quilted textiles. It was Paul D. Pilgrim and their shared love of textiles that brought them together.

Index

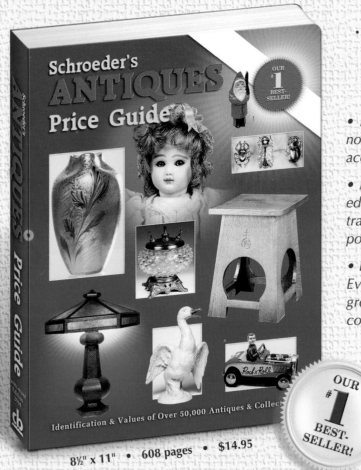
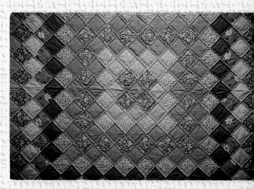